# WHAT OTHERS SAY ABOUT
## *THE ONE AND ONLY YOU*

"Bruce Larson, that fantastic 'people person,' has done it again! This caring Christian continually brings hope to daily living. . . . We've all heard many of the clichés that have to do with each of us being 'one of a kind'. However, in *The One and Only You* a really hope-filled perspective is explored in that we all have the unlimited potential of the liberating security of God's love to draw upon. This book is one of a kind."

*Manhattan Kansas Mercury*

"This book will be appreciated especially by those who wish to discover self through group activity, or by leaders of such groups. It is a 'How-to' book with appropriate tests for analyzing self. It is directed toward the young, the confused, the depressed, those who wish to change and grow."

*Sisters Today*

"The final chapter is worth the whole book. It's called, 'Give Hope Away,'—a wonderful prescription for today."

*The Christian Home*

"The most relevant book of the year!

"This book is vital for spiritual growth. Dr. Larson brings into clear focus the basic insights of spiritual, intellectual, and emotional growth more than any book this reviewer knows of. It is frank, forthright, and fantastic. For the person who is interested in growing emotionally, spiritually, and personally, this book is a must!"

*The Daily Times,* Gainsville, Ga.

*CHOICE BOOKS*
*THE BEST IN FAMILY READING*
P. O. Box 706
Goshen, IN 46526
*We Welcome Your Response*

# THE ONE
# AND ONLY
# YOU

## BRUCE LARSON

A KEY-WORD BOOK
WORD BOOKS, Publisher
Waco, Texas

**THE ONE AND ONLY YOU**

**A KEY-WORD BOOK**

Published by Pillar Books for Word Books, Publisher

*Copyright © 1974 by Bruce Larson*

*First Key-Word Book edition, July 1976*

*Scripture quotations are from the Revised Standard Version of the Bible, copyright 1946, 1952, © 1971, 1973 by the Division of Christian Education of the National Council of the Churches of Christ in the United States of America, and are used by permission.*

*Library of Congress catalog card number: 73-91549*

*ISBN #0-87680-870-4*

*Printed in the United States of America*

To Charles Williams
 Enabler
  Catalyst
   Dreamer
And my friend

# Contents

# Acknowledgments

The author is deeply indebted to the following people:

To my wife, Hazel, for major rewriting and editing;

To Floyd Thatcher and his editorial colleagues at Word for believing in this book and its author and for all of their help in preparing it for publication;

To Keith Miller and Lyman Coleman for reading this book in manuscript form and for giving suggestions and encouragement;

To Loretta Germann for patience, encouragement and typing.

# Forewarned

IF YOU believe in God, it is not too difficult to believe that he is concerned about the universe and all the events on this earth. But the really staggering message of the Bible is that this same God cares deeply about you and your identity and the events of your life.

So, this is a book about you and your uniqueness. It is also about God and the hopeful nature of his love for you. But most of all, it is a book about newness and the possibility of change. This area of newness and change is one in which most of us have difficulty. So before going any further it might be helpful for you to take the following test.

This test is one way to measure your own ability to change and your willingness to change. There are ten questions each requiring a yes or no answer. Give yourself ten points for each yes answer. If you score less than 70 percent, perhaps you can give this book to a friend or save it for some time later in your life.

*CHANGE INDEX TEST*

1. Have you changed your hair style in the last five years?

2. Do you enjoy the opportunity of eating some kind of food that you have never tried before?

3. Do you enjoy making new friends?

4. Have you voted for someone other than the candidate of your political party in the last ten years?

5. Have you switched to any new clothing styles in the last five years?

6. If you moved to a new town would you consider joining a church of a different denomination than the one to which you presently belong?

7. If you attend church services do you welcome innovative styles of worship?

8. Do you find the prospect of a job change exciting?

9. If some circumstance required it, would you find the move to a new town a challenge?

10. Can you hum the tune or recite the words of any popular song written in the last year?

If you scored at least 70 this book is for you. It is my hope that you are ready right now to discover the one and only you.

# 1

## Potential for Newness

IN FEBRUARY of 1973 a man was working on his farm in Wisconsin when suddenly something dropped out of the sky onto the field near him. It was blue, pockmarked, frozen, and mysterious. Excitedly, he chopped off a huge chunk, put it in his deep freeze, and called the sheriff and some geologists from the nearby college to examine it.

For a long time they were all stumped. Was it a meteor? Was it a piece of glacier carried by the jet stream? The only thing they were sure of at the time was that it was frozen hard, and when it melted, it smelled terrible! Much later, someone solved the mystery. It turned out to be blue "potty fluid" accidentally ejected from an airplane toilet.

You know, if I were that man who had received that mysterious gift from heaven, I would probably have done just what he did. I would gather up as much of it as I could to preserve in my deep freeze. And I suspect that over the years a great many things have dropped into my life from out of the blue that I have treated just like that. I have assumed that everything that seems to come from heaven is a gift of God.

So many of our customs and traditions are like that. Sometimes even the life-style or vocation in which we find ourselves fits that category. A family business left by a generous father or a vocation chosen by a well-meaning mother can turn out to be smelly, frozen, and pockmarked and not God's gift at all.

The tragic person is the one who will preserve his freezer full of "blue ice" at all costs and defend it against all charges. Probably everyone has a freezer full of such ice cubes, but one should be able from time to time to examine what he is preserving and eliminate that which seems unnecessary or harmful. However, this calls for change— a painful process for most of us.

Why do we resist change? Why is it painful? It seems to me that most of us find change difficult, if not almost impossible, because of our preoccupation with preserving or defending the past. Actually, the Copernican revolution is a classic example of this tendency.

You will recall that Copernicus came up with the idea that there was a basic flaw in their understanding of the whole astronomical system. He said, "Gentlemen, let me suggest that the sun doesn't revolve around the earth; the earth revolves around the sun."

It took him seventeen years to perfect the theory, and another thirteen years to find a printer who would publish it. It wasn't until after his death that this basic truth was accepted.

If you consider yourself a reactionary, you're in good company. The great churchmen of those days ridiculed Copernicus. Martin Luther said, "This fool will turn the art of astronomy upside down. . . . The Scripture shows and tells another lesson, where Joshua commanded the sun to stand still, not the earth." John Calvin asked, "Who will venture to place the authority of Copernicus above that of the Holy Spirit?" The Vatican damned the Copernican theory as both "philosophically false and formally heretical."

For some reason there is a tendency among Christians to want to look back—to glamorize the past or hold to some outmoded truth, even using the Bible as the authority for preventing change. We are caught in the tension between preserving the good from the past and embracing the new.

Almost seventy years ago, William James, one of America's great pioneer psychologists, said, "Any new theory first is attacked as absurd; then it is admitted to be true, but obvious and insignificant; finally—it seems to be important, so important that its adversaries claim that they themselves discovered it."

What he says so beautifully here is that each of us has in him a bit of the reactionary—some of us to a marked degree. Why is it that some people see themselves primarily as museum keepers, preservers of the past?

A dear friend of mine lives in the most fantastic old house I have ever seen. In it are the accumulated possessions of four generations of people. The house itself is a museum, and it holds a priceless heritage in terms of antique furniture, paintings, and memorabilia.

That house was built by a merchant prince who had once been a penniless boy. He bought the land, built the house, and began to fill it with treasures. Now, four generations later, his heirs see their role as that of preserving and maintaining all the wonders. In a way this is all right; however, there are bound to be new pioneers coming along in that bloodline who refuse to be saddled with the preservation and maintenance of what others have built. It is inevitable that at least one of those great-great grandsons or daughters will become a pioneer of the future, acquiring new lands, seeking new methods for meeting fresh opportunities. And then the cycle will doubtless repeat itself as coming generations see themselves as museum keepers and custodians of the past.

Why are we so resistant to change? Why is change so difficult for each of us? We find one clue in the fact that Jesus likened us to sheep and, if this is true, perhaps this may be one of the reasons we have difficulty with change.

I had a marvelous letter from a friend of mine the other day. In it she wrote, "John was gone for a week, helping his brother's family move to Mississippi and yours truly was left in charge of a flock of pregnant sheep. Believe me, that bit we teach the little ones about little lambs covered with fluffy cotton, running gaily across the greensward is pure hokum! Any similarity between that and raw reality is purely coincidental!

"Never again can I think of the Good Shepherd without knowing that he must love us beyond measure if we are like sheep to him. A sheep is smelly, with an oily kind of dirt that lingers on anything it touches and soaks right through clothing to give an overall aroma long after you've come in. One old ewe that I hate with a passion, since she takes advantage of every unsuspecting moment to assert her authority, had trouble having her lamb. Would you believe we had to pen her up all the while she was trying to incapacitate us (we raise hammer-headed Suffolks) and then rassle her down and sit on her head before we could pull the lamb? Then she was so exhausted she didn't want to get up to take care of her baby, so I pretended to get back into the pen with her and she was so anxious to clobber me, she got up with no trouble at all. And that was only one of seven we delivered that week! Thank heaven the others were less traumatic."

Well, if Jesus calls us sheep and this is what sheep are like, stubborn, hostile, and self-willed, we begin to understand what our problem is as seen through his eyes.

But whether we are basically innovators or reactionaries, there is no possibility for health or life without change. But not all change is good. Some change is unhealthy and a mark of decay and deterioration.

Recently, profound medical and psychological effects of change have been uncovered. Dr. Thomas H. Holmes of the University of Washington School of Medicine has been working with Dr. Richard

Rahe to measure these effects. Holmes rated each life-change event such as the death of a loved one, a change of jobs, moving to a new home, etc., according to the amount of impact such an event would have upon a person's life. His study proved that when too many changes come to any person at any given time, the resulting trauma produces physical illness and even death.

The human body and mind and spirit simply cannot handle too much change at one time. And in the past thirty years we have all had to handle so much change that it is no wonder we talk nostalgically about the good old days. Everything around us is changing so radically.

Recently, I read that the U.S. Agriculture Department has figured out a way for cows to produce milk that is high in polyunsaturated fats. This was achieved by a certain regulation of the cow's diet; they claim the same process can produce beef that is high in polyunsaturated fat. However, there is one major drawback. The milk "tastes like cardboard." The researchers assume that beef produced in the same way will also taste like cardboard.

Any successful marriage is constantly undergoing change. But, again, not all change is necessarily good. My friend Art Sueltz illustrates this by telling about the seven stages of a cold in the life of a young married couple. The first year the husband says, "Sugar, I'm worried about my little baby girl. You've got a bad sniffle. I want to put you in the hospital for a complete checkup. I know the food is lousy, but I've arranged for your meals to be sent up from Rossini's. It's all arranged."

The second year: "Listen, honey, I don't like the sound of that cough. I've called Dr. Miller and he's going to rush right over. Now will you go to bed like a good girl just for me, please?"

Third year: "Maybe you'd better lie down, honey. Nothing like a little rest if you're feeling bad. I'll bring you something to eat. Have we got any soup in the house?"

Fourth year: "Look, dear. Be sensible. After you've fed the kids and washed the dishes you'd better hit the sack."

Fifth year: "Why don't you take a couple of aspirin?"

Sixth year: "If you'd just gargle or something instead of sitting around barking like a seal."

Seventh year: "For heaven's sake stop sneezing. What are you trying to do, give me pneumonia?"

But with all our resistance to change and all the perils of change, it is nevertheless unavoidable. To live is to change. The opposite of change is rigidity, inflexibility. To be alive is to be dynamic and adaptable. This is true for any person, organism, or movement. Arnold Toynbee says, "Civilization is a movement and not a condition, a voyage not a harbor." Medically, doctors look for movement and activity as a sign that the patient is getting well.

Recently in the Georgetown section of Washington all traffic was stopped near a local boutique where two live people were standing in the window acting as mannequins. The effect was so bizarre and stark that it caused a sensation. People were struck by the spectacle of living people being paid to act like nonhumans. Conceived as a gimmick to sell clothes, it seemed instead to be a tragic parable of what life can become at its worst.

Listen to what C. S. Lewis says about real spiritual life. "A statue has the shape of a man but it is not alive. In the same way, man has the 'shape' or likeness of God but he has not got the kind of life God has." [1]

He suggested that this is precisely what Christianity is about. This world is a great sculptor's shop. We are the statues, and there is a rumor going around the shop that some of us are going to "come to life."

I think that says it all. To live with that kind of hope means that we look forward to a form of spiritual change which will be ours as God's people. I was recently asked to take part in the funeral of a dear friend who experienced this kind of spiritual change.

Al was a great guy who, like us all, had many failings, many problems, and many temptations. But Al had become a new creation. Although once an alcoholic, at the time of his death he had been dry for many years. A.A. saved his life, his health, his marriage. Well, his funeral was packed with people from all walks of life, and as I stood at the door after the service, many people commented about how Al had helped them.

Most of them said something about the fact that they were different people because of him. Some had been helped with alcoholism, others mentioned a healed marriage, and still others said they had found faith in God because of him. I was reminded again about what the message of the Bible is all about. God wants to make us new in such a way that people around us will be helped and healed and become helpers of others. My friend had been that kind of person.

Tom Wolfe, one of our most popular writers, said in 1972, "The old dream of the alchemist was to turn base metals into gold. Today he dreams of changing his personality."

To change one's personality! This is impossible, even with the help of the most excellent psychologist or school. But God gives us the promise and the hope that we can change here and now.

# 2

## *We've Only Just Begun*

ONE EVENING recently I went to pick up some friends for a dinner date at our house. They were staying at a local motel. As I opened the door to the lobby, I felt something sharp on the door handle, and when I picked up the house phone to call my friends a minute later, I realized blood was running off my thumb and splashing on the counter. A rough spot on the door had gouged out a whole chunk of skin.

Hanging up the phone, I rushed over to the reception desk and asked, "Can you girls help me? I've cut my thumb on your door and am bleeding all over your lobby." In no time those two lovely girls produced Kleenex and Band-Aids and had me all fixed up. I was greatly impressed with their efficiency and said so.

"It's nothing!" said one girl. "Actually you're the third person today to cut his hand on that same door." Imagine! And still no one had apparently made any attempt to correct the problem by fixing the door.

Now that's exactly what happens all too often in life. Good people have concentrated too much on the hurts of individuals, while neglecting the conditions that cause the hurts. We still need Band-Aids; but we also need some radical changes in our social, cultural, and ecclesiastical architecture. Perhaps our unwillingness to tackle this task comes from a belief that we are locked into limited lives or limited systems.

Recently I spoke at a dinner meeting in Alabama planned by a creative group of people involved in an innovative counseling center. The topic assigned to me was "We've Only Just Begun." As I pondered the theme and prepared my talk, I found that I was beginning to see the church in our time and history in a new way.

I came to feel that the whole idea of "renewal"

is foreign to what God has in mind for his people. Renewal implies going back to an earlier and a better day. Now, when physicists, chemists, engineers, mathematicians, or astronomers get together, they don't talk about going back to the good old days of Pythagoras, Galileo, or Edison. Rather, they use all the best from the past—learn from it and build on it, but no one ever says, "Let's have a renewal in science." To the contrary, they are looking ahead to see what's out there to be discovered.

In this connection I was thinking recently about my former neighbor from Princeton, Albert Einstein. When he taught at the Advanced Study Center there, he lived next-door to Princeton Theological Seminary. One Sunday when I was returning from church I saw him out walking. He was wearing his usual sweatshirt and sneakers; his long white hair was flying in the breeze. He carried the *New York Times*. I rushed up to him and said, "Good morning, Dr. Einstein." He said, "Good morning." Then we walked side by side for three blocks, and I couldn't think of a thing to say. Finally, I turned in at the seminary and said, "Well, good-bye. I live here." Looking at the seminary buildings, he said in amazement, "You live *here?*" And he shook his head and walked on.

In spite of that frustrating encounter, Albert Einstein will always be one of my heroes. He embodies the kind of thing we're talking about here. Back in 1904 when scientists were propounding the law of the conservation of matter (matter can't be destroyed; they said it just changes form), Einstein, who could hardly pass a course in science or math in his early school years, said, "I don't believe that." And, of course, his research finally led to the discovery that the weight of the two halves of an atom was less than the total. Something called energy was released. Out of that came the famous $E=mc^2$ formula that has ushered us into a new age. All because one man believed that the best ideas hadn't been thought of yet. "We've only just begun!"

I believe that God's best ideas about how life can be lived on this tiny spaceship earth have not yet been discovered. When I was a boy, Tinker Toys were very popular. And I was thrilled to receive a set one Christmas. The picture on my little $1.98 box showed all kinds of fantastic things that could be built, but it was the Ferris wheel that took my eye. However, I discovered that a Ferris wheel required all kinds of spools and spindles that I didn't have, plus a motor! It became obvious that I needed box X-23 which cost $14.00 to make the things I wanted. I was trapped in a limited system and was able to build only a few things because of insufficient materials.

The radical thing I'm suggesting is that God has not given us all of his ideas yet about what it means to be a church, to be human beings, to be husbands, wives, parents, children, teachers or students, citizens or statesmen. I believe God is aching to give us new insights and tools about what it means to be the incarnation of his love so that we will no longer have inadequate spiritual Tinker Toys, but the $14.00 set with a motor! We'll be able to put together personal and social pieces we never dreamed of and begin to mend broken lives all around us.

To be open to change in terms of being a dentist, a doctor, a businessman, a homemaker, a lawyer, a student, a gardener, a plumber, a taxi driver, or whatever, is to believe that the best ways of fulfilling those roles are still in the mind of God. He is waiting for people who are not afraid to change and who will not think in terms of a closed system. The tools we've gotten from our past—our schools, our parents—are not the only tools at hand; the greatest way to do your thing probably hasn't yet been discovered. And I predict it will not be discovered by the "smartest" people in your field because it is likely they are trapped by the system—they are experts in the old. I believe that the best ways will be discovered by expectant, frustrated, ordinary people who can hear and cooperate with God's creative Spirit.

At no point in history have we ever had all the truth and light available in any field of knowledge. Recently I found a news item from Dewsbury, England, dated May 20, 1973. It seems that two sane young women were banished to a mental institution fifty years ago at the request of their parents after giving birth to illegitimate babies. One had been committed in 1921 at the age of twenty-three, and the other in 1928, at age twenty. The director of social services there is quoted as saying that they were confined as "moral defectives" under the mental deficiency laws then enforced. In 1959 when the new mental health laws came into effect, the women could have left the institution, but "they continued to stay on because they had nowhere to go."

Thank God for new laws! But there are still newer laws ahead that will correct many present injustices. Change for societies and institutions, as well as for individuals, requires that we rewrite some basic laws about how people live together. We need not only Band-Aids, but new door handles; not just a new concept of treating illness, but a new concept of what illness really is.

Real faith ought to equip us for a life that is constantly changing. The 1967 *Dictionary of Occupational Titles* compiled by the United States Employment Service, lists twenty-three thousand job categories, of which six thousand were non-existent ten years before. If we are reactionary and fearful of change, we are unequipped to live in a society which is always changing.

In the past few months I heard a lecture by a gifted innovator in the field of education. Dwight Allen is Dean of the School of Education at the University of Massachusetts. In discussing how little we really know about the application of the educational processes these days, he suggested, among other things, that the budget for any new school building ought to incorporate a 10-percent figure for renovation after the very first year, and a like amount for every subsequent year. There is no way, he says, that we can erect a building that will be adequate one or two or three years after it is completed. Only as we recognize that we are in a changing world with changing understandings, insights, and values can we begin to provide for the flexibility needed in educating our children.

Tocqueville attributed the greatness of America to this same attitude of openness and willingness to change. In 1787 he asked a sailor why American ships were built to last for only a short time. The sailor's reply reflected amazing insight: "The art of navigation is everyday making such rapid progress, that the finest vessel would become almost useless if it lasted beyond a few years."

It is so essential that we not confuse God's changeless nature with his constantly changing strategies. The Bible is full of that change, and in every age since, God has had a new strategy for expressing himself—his absolute will and love. A friend of mine once commented on the biblical story about Balaam's ass in this way, "The trouble with the Lord once speaking through a jackass is that every time since whenever an ass speaks people think it is the Lord." It is hard for us to hear God in the unexpected, the unfamiliar, and to be open to the new things he is doing today.

But what are the ingredients of change? What are the elements that enable a person to make peace with change to become an eager participant in the process of change, and even being a change agent?

One ingredient that makes change possible was pointed out by psychologist William James, "Lives based on having are less free than lives based on doing or on being." He seems to be saying here that change comes about through people whose energies are concentrated on "doing" or "being" rather than in the acquiring of "things."

Another ingredient has to do with a kind of security that allows us the freedom to fail. Alvin Toffler, in his *Future Shock*, 1970, says, "Some people for reasons still not clear are pitched at a much higher level of stimulus hunger than others. They seem to crave change even when others are reeling from it. A new house, a new car, another trip, another crisis on the job, more houseguests, visits, financial adventures and misadventures—they seem to accept all these and more without apparent ill effect. Yet close analysis of such people often reveals the existence of what might be called 'stability zones' in their lives—certain enduring relationships that are carefully maintained despite all kinds of other changes.

"One man I know has run through a series of love affairs, a divorce and remarriage—all within a very short span of time. He thrives on change, enjoys travel, new foods, new ideas, new movies, plays, and books. He has a high intellect and a low 'boring point,' he is impatient with tradition and restlessly eager for novelty. Ostensibly, he is a walking exemplar of change. When we look more closely, however, we find that he has stayed on the same job for ten years. He drives a battered, seven-year-old automobile. His clothes are several years out of style. His closest friends are long-time professional associates and even a few old college buddies. . . ." [2]

There are tremendous implications for each of us in Toffler's observation. He sees that some things must be stable for others to be negotiable. But beyond that, if a person has found his true nature, being, and destiny, he can then handle a tremendous amount of change and even innovate some change.

I've learned a great deal about handling change this year from two dear friends. Sid and Louise recently moved to Columbia from Alabama when Sid retired from his business.

Louise is a genuine southern belle who had never done a day's work in her life. Raised by maids, she had never made a bed or a cup of instant coffee, let alone clean a toilet. They are now living in a small apartment and her new task is to learn to cook and keep house. She was making great strides until one dismal morning when all the difficulties and frustrations of the past months tumbled in while she was trying to make their two beds. "Sidney Mohr," she called, "come in here. You see those beds? I am not going to make them. What do you think of that?"

Now Sidney is the kind of person I'd like to be —an unruffled lover. He understood immediately that the issue wasn't beds at all, and so he said gently, "That's all right, dear. We'll sleep in them unmade."

"What do you mean, that's all right?" demanded Louise. "You've never slept in an unmade bed in your life and neither have I, and we're not going to start tonight."

"Well," replied Sid, "we'll go to a motel."

"What if we come back tomorrow and I still don't feel like making the beds?" asked Louise.

"We'll just stay in the motel until you do feel like making them."

At that moment all the rebellion left Louise, and she laughed at the whole infantile struggle against God's present plan for her.

Here is a husband who knew what was really at stake. He was not concerned about beds, but about the emotional and psychological needs of a wife who was handling a great deal of change in a short time.

Finally, perhaps the most essential ingredient of change is hope. John Gardner in his book *Self-Renewal* says, "No society is likely to renew itself unless its dominant orientation is to the future." [3] I think this is true for individual people as well. A person who can handle change best and become an instrument of change is one who believes that things are not getting worse but that God is still in the world and there are great times ahead.

All of us can lose sight of this and be almost overcome with despair. One poet said:

> To whom can I speak today?
> The gentle man has perished,
> The violent man has access to everybody.
>
> To whom can I speak today?
> The iniquity that smites the land
> It has no end.
>
> To whom can I speak today?
> There are no righteous men,
> The earth is surrendered to criminals.

This poem was written four thousand years ago by a man in Egypt who was contemplating suicide.

It suggests that hopelessness is an eternal malady and has nothing to do with the times.

It may be true that things are not as good as they ought to be, but change is possible in me and around me and through me. This is what authentic faith is all about. It seems to me that God is saying to his people today, "Forget the former things. Behold, I am doing a new thing."

# 3

## The One and Only You

AT AN EDUCATIONAL seminar at the University of Massachusetts, the lecturer, Dr. Ken Blanchard, said he was going to test our powers of observation. First, he had us pair off and carefully observe each other. Then we were to turn our backs on our partners and make ten changes in appearance. Finally, we were to re-examine the other person to see if we could discern those changes. But Blanchard brought a new dimension to the exercise when he asked, "How many of you, in making changes, took things off your person and how many of you added things?" As it turned out, in that room of several hundred people almost all of us thought of change as removing something—watches, glasses, sweaters, shoes, socks, and so on. Very few of us added things.

Of course, this simple exercise demonstrated one of our basic attitudes toward change. Most of us have an inborn fear of change because we think it will cause us to lose something. But one of the things I am suggesting in this book is that change can often be God's way of helping us find something or add something to our lives. We have to reprogram ourselves to feel that change can mean gaining rather than losing.

The idea of conversion which has always been so frightening to many is nothing more than God offering us the possibility to change. It is a process of gaining rather than losing. It is not a change whereby we lose our identity, but one in which we find it and become the original and authentic self we were meant to be; the one and only you in the universe.

At every level of a person's life there seems to to a universal conspiracy of conformity. It doesn't matter whether you are religious or nonreligious, educated or illiterate, a rebel or a conformist. There is an innate desire in all of us to conform, if only to a handful of other rebels or to a nonconformist from a prior age (a St. Francis or Thoreau).

Now if God made each person to be unique, a one and only version of that life, then sin is expressed when internal and external forces cause us to lose our uniqueness and become a carbon copy, and usually a poor one, of another person or group. So the change that God offers is one that helps a person to find his true identity, his true personhood, and to become "the one and only."

In studying the factors in personality development and human behavior, two very different trends have emerged in psychology. Sigmund Freud is the father of one: depth psychology. The premise of depth psychology is that deep in the unconscious all people are alike. When you peel off layer after layer of all the things that have accrued in our personalities, we are all motivated by sex, aggression, and fear. Simply put, if we go deep enough, all people are basically the same.

But another school of psychology has emerged: trait psychology, and Gordon Allport is the acknowledged founder. In trait psychology and its many branches, psychologists are saying that since all people are alike in depth, it is the surface traits that are really important. It is in the areas where people are different that we find personality and individuality emerging.

It seems to me that each of these schools of psychology has part of a vital truth. If we have to choose one or the other as the whole explanation of human personality, we have missed the key to understanding the one and only you.

If we adopt the premise of depth psychology and assume that everyone else is just like us, then we begin to project on people around us our own feelings, our own hopes, our own fears. I tend to turn other people off because, having met myself, I think I've met everyone and no one else is really worth meeting. I find myself finishing people's stories because I know how they will end. I become more and more cut off and lonely because I have everyone all figured out. Instead of listening to people, I give advice.

If, on the other hand, I emphasize all those traits that make me different, I begin to feel that "I am unique. There is no one else like me." Operating on that premise I begin to be guarded. I can't let people know who I am because of my peculiarities. I cut myself off from all possibilities of love and relationship, of belonging and being. And the result is disastrous!

You must deal realistically with both the differences and the similarities that make you who you are if you are to discover the one and only you. But at the same time there are ways in which we are almost exactly like every other human being that ever lived: our feelings of fear and insecurity, of inadequacy and aggression, of lust and loneliness. However, the differences that have emerged as a result of your conception—your genes and experiences—make you unlike anyone else who ever lived. Both your differences from others and your similarities to every other human being have made you a unique, unrepeatable miracle.

To discover the one and only you is a twofold task. You must uncover the things in you that are in common with every person, and at the same time, you must discover the unique part of you that makes you unlike anyone else who ever lived.

Let's look now at ways in which you can discover your similarities to others, for discovering yourself in depth is the key to being an effective person and communicator. Coming to grips with our similarities helps us identify with other people and empathize with them. This is what good counseling is all about.

This is the special charisma of really great entertainers. Recently I attended a huge concert where Johnny Cash and his troupe were singing. Seeing him, live, and feeling his impact on an audience is an exciting experience. Johnny Cash is a communicator. Because of his own experiences, he is in touch with his feelings and, consequently, with your feelings. The closing number in the concert was a new song that he had written for a film made in the Holy Land. It was from the story of Jesus healing the blind man. The chorus echoed the blind man's request to Jesus, "Touch me again that I might see."

As Johnny Cash finished a verse, he asked the audience to join him on the chorus. Five thousand people in unison found themselves shouting out a prayer that they might be touched. There must have been all sorts of people in that audience— some who at that very moment needed to pray, wanted to pray and did not know how. Now they were able to pray an authentic prayer in the presence of thousands because of the communicating ability of Johnny Cash.

Somebody in touch with his own particular (and, therefore, universal) feelings strikes an immediate response in other people. It is somehow comforting to know that the feelings we think are particular to us are often universal. Being the parent of teenagers can be a scary affair and sometimes it's a help to know how much our difficulties are shared by all the other parents of teenagers. But a friend from Texas sent me a little piece written by some teenagers which suggests six ways to have a more meaningful and understanding relationship with parents.

## HOW TO RAISE YOUR PARENTS

1. Do not be afraid to speak their language. Try to use strange sounding phrases like "I'll help you with the dishes," and "Yes."

2. Try to understand their music. Play Andy Williams' "Moon River" on the stereo until you are accustomed to the sound.

3. Be patient with the underachiever. When you catch your dieting mom sneaking salted peanuts, do not show your disapproval. Tell her you love fat mothers.

4. Encourage your parents to talk about their problems. Try to keep in mind that to them things like earning a living and paying off the mortgage seem important.

5. Be tolerant of their appearance. When your dad gets a haircut, don't feel personally humiliated. Remember it's important to him to look like his peers.

6. Most important of all, if they do something you consider wrong, let them know it's their behavior you dislike, not themselves.

Well, that kind of writing captures the universal feelings of parents and children and brings instant communication and rapport.

Similarities of behavior that produce unusual phenomena are often an object of study by researchers. The British psychiatrist, Dr. H. A. Lyons, reported in the *British Medical Journal* that the instance of depression and suicide has fallen significantly during the years of rioting in Northern Ireland. He feels that there is a direct correlation between aggression and depression. Depression, sometimes leading to suicide, results when aggressive impulses are inhibited. Dr. Lyons says that the suicide rate for Northern Ireland has declined by one-half during the civil strife. Those areas of Belfast hardest hit by violence show the least instance of depression. But in County Down, the most peaceful area of the country, depression continues to rise. If this is true for Northern Ireland, it has implications for most of our Western world. It seems to me this is an invaluable piece of research that can eventually result in a therapeutic way to handle aggression and depression.

At the Child Evaluation Center of the University of Southern California Medical Center, Dr. Edward Lenoski has been researching the questions "Why do people beat their children? Are they insane? Are they pathological? Are they alcoholics?" By studying child beaters he has come up with some interesting similarities. With the exception of a very small group of parents who are definitely psychotic, child beaters are normal people who are unable to share their emotions with others and who express their frustrations in violence. Dr. Lenoski found one characteristic common to all. They were isolationists; they trusted no one and could not share their problems with anyone.

He says child beaters can be rehabilitated, but not by prison terms or professional counselors. Here is his advice, "If you hear your neighbor mercilessly beating her child, it is usually better not to call the police. If you can, try to engage your neighbor in conversation. Say to her, 'It sounds as if you are having a lot of trouble. Is there something I can do to help you?'" He continues, "If that doesn't work, the rights of the child take precedence over everything else and the neighbor must call in someone in authority."

Another fascinating piece of research has been done on the town of Rosetto, Pennsylvania. During the 1960s, Rosettans ritually sat down to meals that would send most doctors reaching for their blood pressure gauges and electrocardiogram machines. Yet not one person under forty-seven ever had a recorded heart attack. Rosettans seemed to eat more and to live longer than everyone else.

But now the doctors say, "The so-called miracle of Rosetto is over. The town's heart attack rate soared to three times the national average last year." And the blame, according to those who tried to explain the phenomenon, lies in the fact that Rosettans, for better or worse, are being "Americanized." The local priest in town says, "We have joined the rat race." And a comment from another community leader: "In 1961 I never saw a Rosetto family sit down to a meal where everyone wasn't at the table together. Now they run in, grab something to eat, and run out again."

Another person says, "They used to confide in each other and share their problems and pleasures. Now they compete to show they are doing better than each other."

It seems that the people who are having heart attacks are the younger generation who work under pressure and sit around worrying about how much money they make. They now commute long distances rather than staying at home and they are chronically in debt.

Dr. Bruhn, who was conducting the research, contends that while cholesterol is still a significant factor in heart attacks, it does not play the major role. "We have found here and elsewhere that many heart attack victims are essentially loners who have nowhere else to turn when the pressure is on,"[4] he concludes.

Well, a sensitive researcher is someone who works with the similarities between people—the common needs, the common drives that make us either sick or well. But how significant that both of these research items indicate that people who are loners have problems. One of the great priorities of the church in our time is to help people discover a community that will foster the kind of fellowship to aid child beaters, potential heart attack victims, and so on.

How tragic that this kind of community is so elusive. Perhaps this is because we are uncertain of the ingredients necessary to create community. A recent experience helped me enormously to understand what some of those ingredients might be. I was part of the faculty for a seminar for church leaders who were going to spend two weeks cruising the Caribbean visiting mission stations and studying relational theology. We had been told in advance that buses would be waiting at the airport in Miami to take us directly to our ship. I boarded a bus in which there were possibly a dozen people all heading for the *Starward*. What we didn't realize, as we started off, was that because of a bus drivers' strike, we had a scab driver.

That bothered some of us who are sensitive about the church's witness in labor relations. But it bothered all of us when we learned that our driver did not know the way to the ship. He got hopelessly lost, took us dozens of miles out of our way, and stopped frequently to radio headquarters to find out where he was and where he should go. As the hour drew near for departure, we became increasingly nervous and fearful. But the amazing thing is that somehow this made us a very tight-knit, loving and supportive community. In fact, those of us who shared that crazy bus ride had something special going for us during the remaining two weeks on the boat.

What were the ingredients of that bus trip? Well, as I've analyzed it, there were six—all essential to genuine community. First of all, there was adventure, and we all respond positively to adventure. Shared adventure builds fellowship. Next, there was worry and fear at various levels which were openly communicated. When people are worried and fearful together, a kind of mutual dependency is created. Third, we had a common problem. We were all lost. A common problem inspires a sense of fellowship. Fourth, we had a need for each other. We gave encouragement and support to each other. Fifth, we had a great sense of fun. This had probably never happened before and would never happen again, and we were involved in something that would never be forgotten. Sixth, our leader had the grace not to pretend that he knew where we were going—he was honest about being lost and involved us in the whole process. We were participating with him in searching for a solution.

I think this says a good deal about the kind of community the church is striving for and the role of the clergy in that community. They are the drivers of our ecclesiastical bus, and they need to let us know when they are lost so that together we can share the adventure and participate in the whole fearful and exhilarating prospect of being the people of God on mission.

Well, let's sum up this whole area of discovering yourself in depth, of finding that part of you which is just like everybody else. The thing that makes you negotiable to the whole world is the knowledge of yourself in depth, of the fears and motivations which make you so much like every other person, whatever color, race, creed, or philosophy.

For me, Hermann Hesse has summed it up beautifully in his *Siddhartha,* written in 1922, "Is this what you mean? That the river is everywhere at the same time, at the source and at the mouth, at the waterfall, at the ferry, at the current, in the ocean and in the mountains, everywhere, and that the present only exists for it, not the shadow of the past, nor the shadow of the future?" "That is it," said Siddhartha, "and when I learned that, I reviewed my life and it was also a river, and Siddhartha the boy, Siddhartha the mature man and Siddhartha the old man, were only separated by shadows, not through reality. Siddhartha's previous lives were also not in the past, and his death and his return to Brahma are not in the future. Nothing was, nothing will be and everything has reality and presence." [5]

Part of the one and only you is universal. It says with Siddhartha, "You are past, you are present, you are future, you are part of all men everywhere in all times." We must not be afraid to plumb that universality that is in each of us which, as we share it, opens doors wherever we go.

However, the other essential part of you consists of those surface traits that you have acquired so painfully for so many years. It is those differences that make you unique and unlike anyone else who ever lived. This also is a part of the one and only you. There is no way that anyone can enter into this part of your life unless you let them. In discovering those things that have made you what you are, the important thing is to make peace with your past, which means everything up to the moment before you read these words. Don't ever evaluate it. Whether it is good or bad, whether you suffered at the hands of outrageously unfair people or were blessed out of all proportion, these things have made you what you are and have shaped the traits and characteristics that make you unlike everyone else.

Let me now give you an exercise that may trigger your thinking about some of the forces that have come into your life to shape the one and only you today. Spend as long as you want on these twelve questions. You can go back to them if you wish, and you may find it helpful to share your answers with a friend or a small group. But the main thing is to begin to accept the things that have happened, both good and bad, that are responsible for you being the one and only you that you presently are.

1. What was your favorite room in your house when you were a child? Why? Try to remember the things that happened there—some of the sights and smells and sounds and people who came to that room.

2. Complete this statement: "One thing I missed during my childhood was _____."

3. What was the best advice you ever received?

4. Which teacher was the most influential in your life and why?

5. Excluding the Bible, what book has made the greatest impression on you?

6. If you could relive one day in your life, which one would it be?

7. What is the most childlike quality that you have retained?

8. What is there about yourself that you joke about most frequently?

9. If you could have one day off unexpectedly next week, how would you spend it?

10. What is the most sentimental possession you have?

11. Of all the material possessions you have, which one gives you the most pleasure?

12. Name the one quality or characteristic you like best about yourself.

Well, these are just starter questions. They should help you lower your bucket deep into the well of your past experiences and present feelings. The one and only you is the product of thousands and millions of forces and interactions and feelings.

This means that you and I then are a strange combination of uniqueness and universality. You are like everybody who ever lived, and you are unlike anyone who ever lived.

# 4

## *God Knows Your Name*

IT SEEMS that I never lose my little kid's sense of anticipation for what the daily mail might bring. Usually it's bills or bulk mail or endless printed things. But on the good days I find a letter from an old friend, from one of our kids away at school, or a letter of appreciation from someone who is reading one of my books.

One of those welcomed letters came recently from a minister in Grand Rapids, Michigan. We had never met, but it seems that while he was reading *Ask Me to Dance*, his seventeen-year-old son was killed in an automobile accident. This new friend went on to tell me how the book had been a needed reminder for him and his wife of God's love and resources in this time of grief. He enclosed a copy of a letter he had written to his son on the day that he was born which was to be opened on the boy's eighteenth birthday—the birthday they would now never celebrate.

The letter tells this new little boy of his parents' feelings as they anticipated his arrival and of their excitement about his birth. It goes on to talk of their hopes and dreams for his future and ends with these two wonderful paragraphs: "There are so many things that I should like to say to you today, bits of advice and words of suggestion for the life that awaits you. Suffice it all to say that you and your wonderful mother have made me the happiest man on earth. I have literally been walking on air! Even forgot early this morning when in Paynesville on business that parking meters had a purpose until I saw a motorcycle cop coming down the street. That fine of one dollar, my son, is your first cost to me! I laughed like mad and surrendered the dollar willingly to the court. For you were worth more than a buck to me, you were worth a million and then some!

"And now, you and I will be entering into a

father-son relationship! Difficult sometimes, to say the least. I, too, had a father; and I know that I was a rascal on more than one occasion—and knowing that you will be a 'chip off the old block,' I predict the same for you. And on the other hand, sometimes, I'll be a bit overbearing and somewhat of a problem to you; but do please bear with me. I know how wonderful your mother is—she'll be a referee deluxe and ever do her best to make our home always 'home, sweet home.' No matter what comes in the course of the years, might this passage from the parable of the prodigal son, where the father speaks to his elder son, ever govern and guide and guard that relationship between us. 'My son, you and I are always together' (Luke 15:31). 'Always together' in life and death, let us be."

I was deeply touched by this father's letter written seventeen years ago, and I wish that I had had the foresight to write such a letter to each of my own three children when they were born. It can be a priceless gift. In fact, I have a similar letter written to me by my father the day before he died. I was eighteen and in the army during World War II. He was in St. Luke's Hospital in Chicago facing surgery. He wrote telling something of his dreams for me and of what he hoped we could do and be together when the war was over.

I still have and treasure my father's letter. Somehow it was a key to who I was at a time when I wasn't certain about much of anything. Before I found God it represented my firmest grip on the mystery of my own identity. Somehow I was the person my father told me I was. Erik Erikson, the great psychoanalyst and self-educated philosopher, has given us the term "identity-crisis." But long before Erikson, man has known that the great quest was his own search for identity. The man of faith knows that his search for himself is inextricably bound up with his search for God.

You see, the biblical revelation of God is in essence the fact that God knows your name. And at the very moment of your birth, and even before, when you were only a thought in your father's mind or a seed in your mother's womb, God knew your name and wrote you a letter. In part he says, "John (Jane), there is nobody else like you. Nobody with your genes. Nobody with your past or potential experience. Nobody who will have your parents, your friends, or your influences. You are the one and only you that I made and I want to tell you who you are." Your letter from God is like the one he wrote to Jeremiah, "Before I formed you in the womb I knew you" (Jer. 1:5). But it is tragic that so many people never read the letter God wrote to them before they were born. They are like my new friend's son who died before reading the beautiful and moving letter that his father wrote.

It is in finding the letter God wrote to you and to no one else that you find yourself in all of your unique and mysterious personality. The tragedy of so many people today can be summed up in the phrase, "I am a wandering generality." I believe it is possible for a person to find God and still not find himself. But I do not believe that you can find yourself truly without finding God.

The message of hope that we have is that God loves us and knows our names. He has written you a letter, and faith is trusting God enough to let him show you this letter. The Bible corroborates this again and again. Jacob has his life changed while wrestling with the angel at the brook Jabbok. There God gives him a new name, "Israel," which means prince. From that moment on Jacob was a new man.

At the scene of the Burning Bush God called Moses by name, and his life was radically changed as he was called to new leadership. And to prove that he is, in fact, God, he calls you by your name. Hearing someone whose very inflections indicate that he knows you demonstrates that this is not man, but God himself.

Samuel, who became a great prophet, first encountered God directly when he heard his own name in the dark of night. God called repeatedly, "Samuel, Samuel." The old priest, Eli, finally understands who is calling and instructs the boy to respond the next time he hears his name by saying, "Your servant heareth, Lord."

When the Apostle Paul meets the risen Christ on the Damascus Road, the first thing he hears is his own name: "Saul, Saul, why do you persecute me?" Over and over again the authenticating mark of God speaking to us is that he uses our name or gives us a new name or speaks to us as the One who knows us and holds the key to our identity. And so, finding God is coming home.

The newspaperman Robert G. Kaiser tells about an American who vacationed in Tbilisi a short while ago. A friend in New York had suggested that while he was there he might look up a certain Russian journalist from the province of Georgia. Installed in his hotel, the American called the journalist. "What are you doing tonight?" the Georgian asked. "Nothing," responded the American. "Stay right there. We'll pick you up in half an hour." The journalist and his wife drove the American and his companion to a restaurant in the hills outside of Tbilisi and ordered a traditional Georgian banquet. Hours later, as they finished the last of many courses and prepared to leave the restaurant, the Georgian turned to his American guest, "I didn't understand you on the telephone. Who did you say gave you my name?"

Mr. Kaiser insists that is a true story. At any rate, I would like to think so because for me it is a parable of what it is like to find God. If you think Georgians are notorious for their hospitality —try God's! The prodigal son coming home doesn't have to tell about all the humiliation, the failures, and the hurts of the far country. He doesn't even have to promise he'll stay home and be good. He finds a loving welcome from someone who is glad to see him and who asks no questions.

Now salvation is a different thing for each person. The God who loves us greets each of us in a different way. Each homecoming is different because our needs are different. Some of us are shy and feel that we have no worth. To come home may mean finding a father who is extravagant in his praise. Others of us are loud and boastful and coming home means a quiet and loving welcome from a father before whom there is no longer a need to boast or brag.

Alvin Rogness, President of Luther Seminary, was telling some of us at a conference what he thought was the heart of the Christian message. He said, "Christians can proclaim to the world their faith not because they're claiming 'I am a lover,' but rather that 'I am loved.'" That is a liberating thought. To say that we are lovers after God's own fashion would be a presumptuous claim. But no one would feel he was bragging or boasting simply to say he was loved by a God who knew him and forgave him.

If, as Alvin Rogness claims, being a Christian is a proclamation of the fact that we are loved and not lovers, we can get on with this business of discovering our true identity and our uniqueness and stop worrying so much about being "good" people. Strangely enough, most of us are not terribly concerned about other people's goodness, we enjoy them the way they are.

In a wonderful cartoon I saw recently, a princess, garbed in all her splendor, is talking to a prince who is decked out in a brilliant uniform. She looks disgusted, and with her hands on her hips, says to him, "I liked you better as a frog!" There is a lot of truth in that. Most of us find that people with their humanity showing are more winsome than those who appear to be so perfect.

A friend told me one evening at a conference that she had made a fool of herself in her small group. "You know, the more I feel like a frog, the more I act like a princess." I think that's a marvelous insight about us all. The thing that turns people off is not our frogginess, but the fact that we continue to fake it and act like a prince or princess when we're not.

So, the great good news that comes from God is that you are free to come as you are. You come to God as you are, and we come to one another as we are. This is possible because God knows our names and says, "You are O.K.!"

There's no doubt about it: If we have heard this message of hope about our uniqueness and have read the letter that God has written to us from our birth, we are different. I believe there is a part of us that will radically change as we hear this message. But it is important also to remember that there is another part of us which will not change. As I read about Paul and those other characters in the Bible, I am continually amazed at how this double truth reveals itself. Paul, according to his last recorded words in the New Testament, is still the same funny, critical, boastful, imperfect rabbi that we saw the first time he walked onto the stage of the New Testament. But, with all that, he is a tremendously changed person. He has a new vision, a new goal, a new purpose, and, indeed, God gave him the power to heal the sick and raise the dead and convert the gentiles.

Recently my wife and I joined a new small group. During the first session together we were all trying to discover who we were and why we were there. Each person was asked to explain why he joined the group. When my turn came, I thought for a bit and then said that the thing I wanted help in most was overcoming my defensive attitude. I said that if I could really experience God's love and forgiveness—not just in my head where I'm committed to it, but in the very pit of my stomach, I would cease being afraid of criticism. That same night the group began to read in Corinthians. I found part of the answer to my personal quest in the second chapter. Paul says, "The spiritual man judges all things, but is himself to be judged by no one" (1 Cor. 2:15). I saw immediately that if I really believe that I am loved and forgiven by God, then it is God whom I have chosen as my judge. And if I choose him as my judge, no one else can judge me. Which means that no one else can condemn me. I am home free by God's own act. Therefore, criticism is merely criticism. It is not judgment. All too often I have considered criticism, even by friends, as judgment. And, of course, judgment can damn and cripple people. If God is our only judge, and he says, "You are forgiven. You are home free," that is staggering good news.

A dear friend of mine died a short while ago. His name was Overton Stephens, and he was a medical doctor in the Toronto area. Overton and his wife, Lillian, met God on a New York weekend many years ago. Just by chance they visited an office where someone prayed with them and later the same day were invited to a small group where they heard talk about God's power to change people. Their "fun" weekend in New York was permanently interrupted as they began to find a whole new dimension to living.

Since then, Overton Stephens, as a physician and as a lay reader in the Anglican Church of Canada, has been responsible for countless lives being changed. And yet, in one sense, Overton was probably not a very different person after his conversion than he had been before. He always had a zest for life and a sense of humor, but he was erratic and unpredictable. All of his uniqueness and humanity and frailty and exuberance were still there. And yet God's Spirit came to live in this physician, and because of him people were physically and spiritually healed.

I went to his funeral, and it was one of the most joyous affairs I've ever attended! His widow and daughters were wearing white. His son had on a blue blazer and white slacks. Many dignitaries of the Anglican church, including the Bishop of Toronto, were there to honor Overton. One of the pallbearers couldn't come, and at the last minute another friend was pressed into service who was wearing a bright sport coat and plaid slacks. But, I'm sure he was one of God's "plants." For this man had been cured of what was diagnosed as incurable cancer through Overton's prayer and medicine. Here was another proof that the man they were burying was indeed a new creation. A modern day Lazarus was a pallbearer at his healer's funeral!

Was Overton a good man? That's hard to evaluate, and it's beside the point. Was he a new, unique champion of the Holy Spirit? Like few people I have ever known!

Some of the last words that Overton said to me before he died provide a key to this. He said, "Bruce, this has been a great life. You know I believe in the resurrection and in life after death. But even if I didn't, I would still have given my life to God because the life he's given me in this world is so terrific. I wouldn't have missed a minute of it."

Overton found a God who knew his name. He dared to read the letter that God had written about him and for him when he was born. Death for Overton was not terrifying because he found out who he was.

Someone sent me an anonymous poem some time ago. I don't even remember who sent it, but I am indebted to whoever it was for these lines:

> Death is the revealer of all men;
> He tears aside life's thin disguise
> And man's true greatness, long unknown,
> Stands clear before your eyes.

In death we do know truth and become truth in a mysterious and frightening way. But we don't have to wait until we die for this kind of revelation. We can begin now to be who we are and to discover our identity.

In the last few years I put together a polarities test that I've been using with all sorts of groups. This test has been a great icebreaker and an insight giver. It's a test that should help you discover the ways in which you are unlike anyone else. You see, all of life is made up of polarities, and your uniqueness is a combination of thousands of such polarities, a combination unlike anyone else's. Incidentally, when you've taken the test, try it on your spouse or your best friend. The chances are you've been drawn to someone with the opposite polarities. But, opposite or similar, it's unlikely that anyone would have your exact polarities even in these limited areas. I think you'll find the answering of these twelve questions both interesting and helpful. Complete each sentence with the word that best describes you.

## MY POLARITIES

1. I prefer to do my most creative work in the . . .
   ☐ morning ☐ evening

2. I feel most comfortable . . .
   ☐ indoors ☐ outdoors

3. I am usually in the role of a . . .
   ☐ talker ☐ listener

4. I prefer to handle disagreements . . .
   ☐ right now ☐ later

5. I think of myself in terms of a . . .
   ☐ giver ☐ receiver

6. I store my personal belongings with . . .
   ☐ methodical ☐ unstructured
   neatness creativity

7. In new situations I rely on . . .
   ☐ logic ☐ intuition

8. If I have a choice, I prefer to be . . .
   ☐ alone ☐ in a group

9. It gives me great satisfaction to be able to . . .
   ☐ save ☐ spend

10. I prefer to resolve a difficult relationship by . . .
    ☐ letter ☐ telephone

11. In keeping appointments I am usually . . .
    ☐ punctual ☐ casual

12. In terms of starting the new or preserving the old I think I am mostly a . . .
    ☐ museum ☐ explorer
    keeper

Most of us have at some time been criticized for being the people we are in these polarities. I'm suggesting that we quit trying to fake it. Let's say instead that in general this is the kind of person I am. To pretend otherwise makes us hopelessly schizophrenic and defensive. When I can say to people, "This is what I am," and not have to defend myself, I can begin to appreciate the other half of the polarity and, incidentally, become a more well-balanced person. Wholeness comes as I am able to say unashamedly, "This is me. This is what feels the best to me. This is what I have to give God."

Incidentally, I am convinced that as we begin to feel comfortable in our own identity, we stop trying to make other people conform to what we think they should be. Jesus said to Judas on the night of his betrayal, "Do what you have to do." Jesus knew what was going to happen and undoubtedly felt sorry for Judas, but he gave Judas the freedom to do what he had to do, being the person he was at that moment. Love means allowing the other person that freedom even if his irresponsible action leads to a cross for you. That's what Jesus did. He gave Judas freedom, and then Jesus paid the price.

Finding our own identity and our own uniqueness enables us to free the people around us in this same way. This is the mark of a person who has read God's letter with his name on it, who knows that God is saying, "Come as you are. You are loved."

# 5

## *Discover Your Past*

FOR SOME REASON I fear the past. I have always feared the past and would like to bury it, but somehow it won't stay buried. It turned up, for example, at a conference my wife and I attended recently in Chicago. Now Chicago is my hometown, and when I lived there during my teenage years, I wore a variety of masks, none of which was very spiritual.

Well, at this church renewal conference, one of my old high-school buddies turned up. He was surprised and delighted to see me, and I was equally glad to see him. That's the good news. Now for the bad news. As we were reestablishing our long ties, he suddenly turned to Hazel (who is the person to whom I play my life and for whom I want to be a hero) and said, "Did Bruce ever tell you that he was the worst left tackle ever to play on an Evanston High School football team?" Well, that's a hard line to follow, and I suppose bumping into ghosts like that makes me continue to fear the past.

I still have anxious moments when I wake up in the middle of the night and remember things that I've left undone or things done that should not have been. As a child, I recall the dread of being discovered by my family in some of my early sexual fantasies and escapades. But just as painful is the memory of a particular gift I received one Christmas. A very poor old lady who lived in a distant state sent me the incredibly large present of $1.00, a really sacrificial gift for her. Well, I postponed writing my thank-you letter even though my mother reminded me daily. And this dear old adopted "aunt" died early in February, never knowing how much her gift meant to me. My negligence still stirs feelings of guilt, and I can recall waking up in tears those many years ago because I was afraid she did not know. I'm sure this dear old friend now knows all things including my love and gratitude.

Sometimes my recurring nightmares are about taking an exam in grade school or high school for which I was totally unprepared. Imagine, here I am, a middle-aged man, soon to approach senior citizenry and I'm still haunted by thirty-five-year-old dreams of inadequacy and lack of preparation.

Sometimes present events stir up some of these primal memories. Recently I was asked by an old army buddy to come down to his town in Virginia to speak to the annual dinner for the chamber of commerce. It was not until I was introduced at the banquet by my friend that I became aware of the fact that I was the only man in the dining room not wearing a tuxedo. All of my past fears of inadequacy had to be conquered before I could go on with the speech I had prepared. You might not have known it to look at me, but at that moment I had become the small boy from the Great Depression in a hand-me-down suit and it was unnerving.

The second time I spoke at a chamber of commerce dinner I suffered a somewhat different kind of a trauma. An old friend in upstate New York was being honored as the retiring president, and he had asked if I would be the speaker at the event. He informed me that it was a formal affair and added that he hoped I would not pull my usual cheapskate act and wear a clerical collar. So, determined to be prepared this time, I called the local tuxedo rental in our town, gave them my appropriate measurements, and arranged to pick up my finery the morning of my flight. When I went down to pick it up, I discovered that the only tuxedos rented in the swinging new town of Columbia were very "mod" affairs with belted backs and purple lapels. And the shirts were amply decorated with lace. It was too late to do anything about it, so I gathered it all up and headed for the airport. That night before the chamber of commerce in Binghamton, New York, where literally hundreds of people were attired in the traditional "waiter's suit," I was resplendent in my Edwardian tux and ruffles. To make matters worse, it was the first time that they had ever asked a clergyman to speak. "Some way for a spiritual type to appear at a secular banquet!" I thought. And again I had to fight down all the old fears from the past about wearing the wrong thing to a party. You know, if you're equally anxious about being overdressed or underdressed, it's hard to win.

For too long, in the great adventure of trying to discover who I am, I have believed that the past was my enemy. My pattern has been to hurry on, move into the future as quickly as possible, and to get the past behind me because I have believed that it contained the seeds of my undoing. Now, it's true that the past is important, but in a creative way. You don't have to take a short or long course in Freud to know that it is a powerful force in shaping who you are right now. Actually there is no way the past can be ignored in the process of discovering the one and only you.

Several months ago I ran into two old friends whose lives had been radically changed during a lay renewal weekend. I hadn't seen them in some time, and as we sat down to catch up on each other, I heard a wonderful story that taught me much about the power of the past in our lives.

Talking alternately, the two of them began to tell about the great change that had come into their lives since that memorable weekend. But they said, "You know, the change came too late for it to make much of a difference in the lives of our children." Their children, like ours, were now late teenagers. They continued, "We were so unloving and unreal when our kids were young and even though we have changed, their relationship to us is much the same. We began to wish we could have the privilege of parenthood again now that we have new resources, and we finally decided to take training to become foster parents. We got our first little child, Timmy, two years ago. His mother was fifteen and unmarried, and he came to us just after he was born."

When little Timmy came into their lives and home, he was frightened and tense—the victim of frequent spasms. His hands were tightly closed in a fist, and his arms were perpetually wrapped about himself in a hugging position. Understanding something of the trauma that Timmy must have had, Gene and Ellen began to talk to him. "We began to talk to him all the time that he was awake," they said, "and pray for him much of the time when he was asleep."

I was intrigued. These two people had no formal training in psychology, theology, or counseling and yet they were attempting one of the most profound things I had ever heard of. "What did you say to him or how did you pray?" I asked. "Well," they replied, "we talked to his unconscious when he was asleep and to his conscious when he was awake. We said things like 'Timmy, you're beautiful and we love you and we're glad you've come to be with us. Don't be afraid. God loves you and your mother loves you. She had to give you up because she was frightened and in trouble.'" And all the while this tiny child clutched his fists and hugged himself.

But, a turning point came when Timmy was about ten weeks old. Gene, an aggressive and successful salesman (hardly the type I would think of as a foster parent), woke up at six one morning and found Ellen feeding Timmy and talking to him. He said, "Ellen, when you finish, put him in bed with me for awhile." Gene removed his pajama top and Ellen took off Timmy's shirt, and then Gene hugged the little fellow to his chest and began talking to him and rocking him.

When it was time to get ready for work, Gene called Ellen to take Timmy. She said, "No, just lay him on the bed and I'll get him later." When Gene laid Timmy on his back and began to get up, that little baby unclenched his fists and opened his arms in a gesture of vulnerability for the very first time. He had felt love and responded.

They were deeply moved by that first sign of hope. And at six months Timmy was so well he was ready for adoption, which was the arrangement they had agreed to. But when the people who were to adopt him read his records, they were fearful that he would be a problem. To Gene and Ellen's delight they gave him up at the last minute, and my friends were then free to make Timmy their legal son. At the end of this remarkable story they showed me pictures of Timmy, now three years old. A more beautiful, happy, and healthy child I have never seen.

What has all this to do with the past? Well, we have all experienced tremendous trauma as children, babies, even prenatally. But most of us have not had the benefit of parents with the sensitivity and the wisdom to channel God's healing love in the way that Gene and Ellen did. Most of us grow up clutching our fists and hugging our bodies either psychologically or literally. We go through life scarred by all of that early fear. People are guarded and cautious and introverted and shy simply because they've never had parents who were able to minister as Gene and Ellen did, and so few friends are found along the way who can begin to speak to the frightened child inside of us. It seems to me this ought to be a priority for the community of faith; to speak to the "Timmy" inside each of us. We can all be parents to one another and say, "It's O.K. You are beautiful. You are loved. That's the real you. That's the one and only you."

My mother is eighty-five years old, and she is still a vivacious gal, full of spunk and faith. Mother has been a fighter for the causes and things she believes in all of her life, but not until two years ago did I begin to understand part of the dynamic of her life. It was Christmas. We were recounting something about past Christmases when she told me something about herself that I had never known.

I knew that when my mother was born, her mother died and later her father had remarried and fathered ten more children. I also knew that at fourteen she left Sweden to come to America alone to make a life for herself—not knowing the language and having almost nothing going for her. What I hadn't known was that she did not choose to come to America—her father and stepmother sent her. They paid her passage all the way from Sweden to New York, but when the boat stopped in England, she was so frightened that she turned around and went back. Their reaction was to put her right back on the next boat leaving for America.

Well, if I had known this part of my mother's past earlier, I'm sure I could have been much more understanding of the person she was and more appreciative of her adjustment to that traumatic experience. But each of us has had traumas in our lives that account for some of our strange and erratic present behavior. And if we know what the past has been, present behavior begins to make sense.

I recently talked to a gifted doctor who told about an operation he had performed on a four-teen-year-old boy to remove a huge tumor from his eye. He said that the tumor they removed turned out to be the undeveloped embryo of this boy's twin. I had never heard of such a thing, but I have since learned it is not too uncommon. It seemed an especially graphic example of the fact that each of us may carry a tumor inside that is actually a part of the past.

Someone told me that the inventor of penicillin never revealed his invention until a colleague came upon it many years later and released it to the world. Apparently the father of this very famous and gifted research scientist kept telling him as a boy to "keep still!" This so influenced the boy that he found it almost impossible to speak out, even when he had discovered one of the great healing drugs of all time. His father's command to "keep still" caused him to withhold a treasure that, had he felt free to tell others about it, could have saved many more lives.

Well, as you begin the great adventure of discovering who you are, realize that nowhere will you find a better resource than in your past. There is a vast treasure there which can be mined and made to work for you.

Not long ago I stopped by to visit some friends in Columbia, Maryland. A charming woman and her young son were staying with them. This attractive matron charmed all of us, and I made one of my hasty evaluations which prove to be wrong about 90 percent of the time. I assumed she probably had grown up as a hothouse flower and had never known worry, fear, or problems in her life. It wasn't until we'd been together for almost two hours that she began to tell me about herself. It seems that she had married a brutal man who, in collusion with his mother and the doctor, had gotten her committed to a mental hospital where she received both shock treatments and therapy. Ultimately she had been released, her husband had died, and after a time, she remarried. To compound the horror of the whole story she further explained that as a child of twelve she had been left an orphan and was adopted by an aunt and uncle who in no way had made her feel loved.

Finally, I asked her why she was not bitter, frightened, hostile, or paranoid about her past. I don't think she knew quite how to answer. But she did say that since finding God she had become unafraid of her past and now blamed no one. She was excited about her future because she was unafraid to face her past, and she felt no bitterness toward the people who had failed her. Also, she had become a sensitive and caring person because of the hurt and pain she had experienced. Her past had become a treasure she was mining in the present.

This is a model for all of us. We must not label the past either bad or good. All of our past is useful to us. We learn from what has happened to us, and we also learn from the things we have done to other people.

I have received much help from friends of mine who have mined the treasures in their past. I think of Keith Miller who, in his book *Habitation of Dragons*, has been able to help so many of us by delving back into his past and reliving things that have been shut away. Rather than being ashamed and frightened and trying to forget the past, Keith has let the past mold him into a deeply caring person and an able communicator.

My friend, Karl Olsson, has the same gift. It's

a great thing to be at a dinner party with Karl and hear him spin off stories of the tragic and comic things that have happened in his life. So many of the hurts, humiliations, and embarrassments that were a part of his early years have spoken to me of the grace of God in new ways. Karl in his latest book *Come to the Party* has mined some of that gold from his past.

These friends, and others like them, are giving me hope to move into my past, claim it, and use it. Perhaps I can thank God for all of it—not just the good parts where I come off a hero, but even for the parts where I come off with jam on my face. God says that all of my past is okay because I am forgiven. He alone is my judge, and, therefore, the past is mine to enjoy and to use.

How then can the treasure in your past help you to become "the one and only you" that no one else can be? First, we need to walk back into it unafraid. We should walk back knowing that nothing we have done can hurt us now if we believe that we are loved and forgiven. This opens the entire past to us. We don't need to be condemned by our old memories, but we can explore them and use them in building our lives as they are meant to be.

Yes, the shape of our present and our future lies in claiming the past. Blaise Pascal, that brilliant French scientist from the seventeenth century, who gave us such things as the barometer and the adding machine, had a remarkable spiritual experience in his room one night. He called it *Fire in the Night* and wrote about it. He then sewed that written account in the lining of his coat. All the rest of his very brief life he could touch and feel the crinkle of this paper, but he never showed it to anyone. It was discovered after his death.

Pascal understood that sometimes there are things which God gives us that are too intimate to share with anyone. They are a part of us and our past and must be claimed and enjoyed as something he has used to bring us to this point.

But more often we claim the treasure of our past by sharing it with others. Recently my wife and I went through the experience of helping friends bury their twelve-year-old daughter. These are two of our dearest friends, and we were with them all through those hard days of funeral preparations—choosing a casket, picking a cemetery plot, deciding on a service, and all the rest. Then, from time to time after the funeral we would call and say, "How is it going with you?" And they told us how lonely and fearful they were and how at times they doubted that God was really there. A few months later, however, neighbors of theirs lost a daughter in an equally tragic way. Our friends, who up to that point had been unable to receive much comfort, found they were uniquely prepared to help this family. And in sharing with this other couple my friends were able for the first time to claim and use redemptively their own recent tragic experience. This is certainly one way in which God meant us all to use our past.

Finally, we claim the treasure in our past when we give it to God. Somehow we have to let go of those things from the past that are either painful or dear. Karl Olsson frequently says that one of the great acts of faith in the Bible is found in Genesis where Abraham buries Sarah. There we hear Abraham saying, "Give me property among you for a burying place that I may bury my dead out of sight." So often we do not bury the dead "out of sight." We keep them alive in our memory in an unhealthy way. We keep living with the dead to our own detriment. Abraham was able to place his beloved Sarah in the cave of Machpelah to say "our life together is over," and to move on. This is how he honored Sarah. The past is claimed by allowing it to go.

As a young man I had great difficulty accepting my father's death because I was away from home in the army. I hid his death inside me for a long time. My father was cremated, and mother kept his ashes around for many years. Long after Hazel and I established our home mother married a wonderful man. In time my stepfather was able to suggest that he didn't want to live in a house with a former husband's remains. So mother gave my father's ashes to me. At the time, I was living in Binghamton, New York, and I recall vividly the snowy day that I walked out alone in one of our beautiful state parks—a place my father would have loved. I prayed and thanked God for him— who he was and what he meant to me. Then I opened that box and threw his ashes to the wind.

Somehow in that act I "let go of my father," and the scattering of the ashes was to me sacramental and liberating. I am left with the memory of those seventeen years that we shared together.

# 6

## *Live in Your Present*

IT WAS a beautiful fall day in Indianapolis when I stepped off the plane and climbed into a taxi cab. As we were driving along, I remarked to the driver, "It's really a gorgeous day out here in Indiana."

"You should have been here yesterday" was his response. "It was terrible."

We drove a bit further and I said, "You know, most of our autumn leaves are gone in Maryland, but your trees are still beautiful. I'm glad I came this week."

"These leaves will be gone in three or four days," he predicted.

We came alongside the Indianapolis Speedway where the greatest car-racing event occurs every Memorial Day. "Isn't this the Indianapolis Speedway?" I asked.

"Yes," he replied.

"I'd sure like to see the race here some Memorial Day," I said.

"I wouldn't go near it," responded the cabby. When I asked why not, the driver answered, "I'd rather watch the horses run."

"Ah, you go to the track?"

"No, I never go. It's too expensive."

When we parted, I was struck by the hopelessness of this man's outlook. Even the good days are bad because they will soon change. My cab driver's motto seemed to be, "Behind every silver lining there is a dark cloud."

Now, by way of contrast, another friend recently sent me a postcard, apropos of nothing in his great bold scrawl. Here is what it said, "Thought for the day. If you plan to swallow a frog it is best not to look at it too long. If you have a number of frogs to swallow, swallow the big one first." And it was signed, "George." The sender was George McCausland known all over the Pittsburgh area as "Uncle George." He is in demand as a conference speaker, counselor, and encourager of the discouraged.

For "Uncle George" every day is an adventure, and for those who have the privilege of being his friends, that adventure is contagious. You never know when a visit or a phone call or a postcard like the one I received will burst into your day and lift your sights.

The Bible says, *"Today* is the day of salvation. *Now* is the acceptable hour." All this means is that we can only know God in the present tense. Our yesterdays are gone, but they are dynamic fertilizer for everything we do today. We cannot live in tomorrow, though our dreams for tomorrow certainly shape today. Today is the only day that you have to discover the one and only you. You and I make each day what it is. Many of the same experiences may come to all of us and yet find a very different response with each person. However, in a more profound sense, things do not happen to us entirely by chance. They can be the logical outcome of our life-style or attitude.

One morning when I stepped out from my room in a Topeka, Kansas, motel, I was delighted to see that the rain of many days had stopped. The sun was out, and it was a windy, clear, beautiful spring day. As I passed a lovely young lady in the corridor, I said, "It's a beautiful day, isn't it?" She immediately replied, "Yes. And it's about time. We deserve one."

Well, that one remark made me happy that I was not her employer, co-worker, or husband. Her whole attitude toward life and each new day was certainly reflected in her reply.

I think of another old friend who loves to do

favors for everybody, but resists having anything done for him. If he is a guest in your home and you ask him what he wants for breakfast, he says, "Oh, anything. Whatever you're going to have. Whatever you happen to have around." Somehow I get the feeling that it is impossible to please him and perhaps he even welcomes the chance to suffer a little each day.

Another old friend I know loves to tell about the many ways she has fooled her husband: tricking him into something he doesn't want to do . . . eating food he doesn't like . . . getting him to admit that he was wrong and she was right. You get the feeling that each day is seen as a series of contests which she hopes to win.

Then I have a newer friend who impresses me as a kind, considerate, and caring person. But if you ask her how she is, she invariably conveys a tremendous sense of pressure and busyness. She is involved in a number of organizations, and her day is crammed with people's demands. It's almost as though her unavailability was by deliberate plan.

By way of contrast, one of the busiest men I have ever met, always gives the impression when you see him or call him that he has unlimited time for you. I've found that he builds chunks of leisure into his schedule simply in order to be available to the needs of some friend or group. For this friend life does not mean being harried in good works. It is a gift to be enjoyed and shared with others.

A young friend of mine who is the president of a growing company recently told me about a management seminar he had attended, and he shared one of the most important concepts he had gleaned from it. The difference between "good", and "great" leadership really has to do with your attitude toward the day's work. A manager can approach the day with either a "have to" or a "want to" attitude. The idea that anybody ever "has to" do anything is a fallacy. You can always quit your job or leave your spouse or go on welfare. Nobody "has to" stay married or keep his job or even pay his taxes. (He can go to jail!) The executive who communicates to his family and friends and employees that he is always rushing is really a very poor leader. People working under him have the same sense of pressure and drudgery.

I immediately saw that I've been guilty of this same syndrome. My busyness had subtly communicated, "Well, I have to go here or speak there or help with this project." Since then, I've been trying to change so that I can honestly realize that God gives me privileges each day. I only have to do the things I want or choose to do. Each person shapes his own day by his overall attitude and then by screening the events that make up that day.

Part of the key to living in the present is in understanding that all of us are living out some kind of a "game plan." Now a game plan is nothing more than an agreed-upon plan like the one a football team selects to beat the other team. Before the game they must decide if they're going to play primarily a running game or a passing game, a defensive game or an offensive game. Similarly, at an early age each of us has adopted a game plan for handling life. This simply means that we revert unconsciously or consciously to these early instinctual patterns to handle the events of life. As each day comes along, our actions and reactions seem to fit into an overall kind of plan. And to understand your game plan, to accept it or modify it, is essential in discovering the one and only you. As the overall pattern becomes clear, I begin to understand that the way I handle the events of each day is consistent with that total scheme.

Dr. Homer Dodge, an incredible man, lives near Columbia, Maryland. He has a Ph.D. in physics and is president emeritus of Norwich University in Vermont. Dr. Dodge is a writer, explorer, cartographer, adventurer, and probably the world's only eighty-five-year-old white water canoeist. He's been canoeing for over seventy years. For a long time Dodge had wanted to run the dangerous Long Salt Rapids, but he just hadn't gotten around to it. At age sixty-nine, when the construction of the St. Lawrence Seaway threatened to quiet the rapids forever, he took the plunge. He is the only person to run that stretch in an open canoe since the early fur traders.

When a reporter asked him recently the secret of his adventuresome life, he replied, "If you want to have interesting experiences, put yourself where they can happen. By ranging around I have put myself where luck and experience could find me."[6] Each day that this delightful adventurer has lived has been an extension of an overall, conscious game plan.

Recently I was talking to the daughter of a close friend about one of the men she had been dating for a long time. I asked if she would ever marry him and was surprised by her answer: "No, I don't think so. I tried hard to make it work, but he was such an unhappy and a 'not O.K.' person that I knew I could never handle it." Then came the shocker. She added, "You know, I think I'm a lot like you. My game plan is to try to make other people happy. This can be a terrible tyranny. The more I tried to make John feel okay and happy, the worse I felt about myself. I kept saying, 'You're a failure. If you were everything you ought to be, then he'd feel great.' " Then came a remarkable bit of wisdom. "You know," she said, "I finally realized that I can't make anybody else happy. I can only share my happiness or my sorrow with someone else. It's not in my power to make another person happy. But with my game plan, I will only make myself miserable if I marry an unhappy person."

At still an early age this young woman has come to understand something of the game plan that she is stuck with, and she is learning to work creatively with it. Possibly none of us can greatly change our game plan, but to understand what it is and how it works can be liberating.

I have a great friend down in Montgomery, Alabama, and a few years ago he told me an unforgettable story of a summer vacation he had planned for his wife and children. He was unable to go himself because of business, but he helped them plan every day of a camping trip in the family station wagon from Montgomery all the way to California, up and down the West Coast, and then back to Montgomery.

He knew their route exactly and the precise time they would be crossing the Great Divide. So, my friend arranged to fly himself out to the nearest airport and hire a car and a driver to take him to a place which every car must pass. He sat by the side of the road for several hours waiting for the sight of that familiar station wagon. When it came into view, he stepped out on the road and put his thumb out to hitchhike a ride with the family who assumed he was 3,000 miles away.

I said to him, "Coleman, I'm surprised they didn't drive off the road in terror or drop dead of a heart attack. What an incredible story. Why did you go to all that trouble?"

"Well, Bruce," he said, "someday I'm going to be dead and when that happens I want my kids and my wife to say, 'You know, Dad was a lot of fun.'"

Wow, I thought. Here is a man whose whole game plan is to make fun and happiness for other people.

It made me wonder what my family will remember about me. I'm sure they will say, "Well, Dad was a nice guy but he sure worried a lot about putting out the lights and closing the windows and picking up around the house and cutting the grass." But I'd also like them to be able to say that Dad was the guy who made life a lot of fun.

This business of understanding your own game plan and the endless variety of game plans other people work under is an essential key to discovering ourselves and to helping other people understand who they are. And as I see it there are three questions that are relevant to recognizing our own game plan:

1. First, how do you see yourself? What do you think your game plan is? What is the thing you're trying to accomplish day by day as you relate to others? Since none of us can radically change our game plan we have to learn to recognize and work with our consistent patterns and responses. Perhaps you identified with one of the people I've mentioned: the cab driver who sees the worst side of everything; the young lady who deserves anything good that happens to her; the woman who makes each day a contest she plans to win; the man who enjoys a martyr's role. Unless we can recognize our game plan, it's often difficult to be open to God's guidance. It is hard to feel God is leading you into comfortable circumstances if you welcome suffering. If you enjoy being pressured

and harried, it's hard to hear him say no to any new assignments.

2. How do people see you? What kind of a game plan do you communicate? What do they think are your goals and values and interests? Probably the best way to find out is simply to ask them. A small group can be an ideal place to get a helpful response to the questions: "How do you see me? How do I come across? What do you think my game plan is?"

3. How do you see other people? How do you work with them in their game plan in a way that is helpful to them? Effective leadership and counseling surely depend on this.

Now, how does our game plan develop? It begins in our very early months and years of life as we learn how to handle trauma. If you are a parent you have a special appreciation for the kind of game plan which babies and small children develop from very early years.

We have two sons. One was born saying no! He questioned everything and rebelled against authority in general and against school and haircuts in particular. In high school he led active protests against the war in Vietnam, the examination system, and even the junior prom. But as an adult, his rebelliousness seems to have taken some very creative forms.

Our other son has handled trauma in quite a different way. He has made friends with the world and almost everybody in it. If I am in trouble, I enjoy being with him for he never has to lay blame. I remember several frightening experiences on our boat when it came very close to sinking. When the rest of the family was saying, "Dad, how did you ever get us into this mess?"

he would encourage me, "Don't worry. It will be O.K. We'll get out."

Very early both boys learned how to handle life and its traumas with a completely different game plan. And that game plan carries over consistently into their adulthood even as it does with you and me.

It is helpful for us to remember that the variety of game plans people develop is endless. There are the withholders—they never give praise or thanks or approval or pitch in voluntarily . . . the sulkers . . . the fighters . . . the rebels . . . the people pleasers . . . escapists who hide behind some habit or activity where they won't be found.

In finding ways to handle trauma or the fear of being rejected and hurt, we adopt the style which becomes our game plan for life. That in itself is neither good nor bad. Rather, it is part of our uniqueness, of our originality.

Another shaping force in our game plan is the fact of our own egocentricity. Each of us sees life, not as it actually is, but as a drama with ourselves in the role of the hero. John Barth, in *End of the Road*, calls this "mytho therapy." For example, at a wedding the bride sees herself as the central figure with all the rest of us, including the groom, the minister, and the parents, as supporting players. But each guest who is there, no matter how distant a relative or friend, sees himself or herself as the central figure. The wedding becomes a background for his life that day.

Perhaps this explains why employees in an office can take major upsets or reverses with much less seriousness than does the president. They see their own personal lives as central. The company is incidental and is simply a means of making a livelihood and "doing their thing." But, the president or the chairman of the board sees himself and the company as central—the employees are merely bit players. This same egocentricity probably explains why children don't take the responsibility for their homes very seriously. The home, which is central to the parent, is only background music for the drama of the child's life where he and his interests are center stage.

It is interesting to understand that our game plan is consistently most apparent in moments of panic and stress. For example, imagine yourself in the following situation.

You have run out of gas on a deserted road in the middle of the night. The nearest help is at least ten miles away. What is your first reaction as your car comes to a halt?

Now, I'm not asking how you would handle the problem. That is a different matter entirely and depends on logic, training, and so on. I'm asking you to describe the feelings in your stomach the moment your predicament becomes apparent.

The immediate reaction of some would be to blame another person: "How come my wife never checks the gas tank!" Others would instantly blame themselves: "Larson, you stupid idiot. You've done it again." Some would panic: "Great Scott. I just read this morning that crime is on the increase in this area. I may never get out of this alive." Others would withdraw: "If I just go to sleep now, I'm sure help will come by in the morning." Still others would immediately rationalize that things are not so bad: "This is certainly going to teach me a lesson, and I can finally put my boy scout training to work. Besides, it's going to make a great story later."

There are at least fifty more possible gut reactions. Try to find yours and know that this same feeling reaction will influence your behavior in most crisis situations. In one sense, each of us is a product of what a great many people have done to us. In another sense, we can choose daily with certain limits what our game plan will be. The important thing is that you understand who you are and that you enjoy being who you are . . . the one and only you.

# 7

*Claim Your Future*

DO YOU recall the chapter from *The Adventures of Tom Sawyer* where Tom and Huck are spectators at their own funeral? I had a similar experience recently through a letter written to my office. The writer had just heard a rumor that I had died, and she was expressing her grief and extending her sympathy to my colleagues. And she said some very nice things—things that I was very pleased to hear while still a part of this world.

To read a letter full of praise and eulogy and sadness over your death is a beautiful experience. It was premature, happily. But it made me aware that my death is already certain.

Recently I heard a speaker say, "Make no mistake about it. God means to kill us all." Nevertheless, we all somehow feel that our own death is either impossible or so far in the future that it is irrelevant. This speaker was reminding us that we have no choice at all about our eventual death. God has created a system that makes it inevitable for all life. But we can choose our attitude towards death and, in some measure, the circumstances of our death. And we do have total choice in how we live the days, weeks, months, or years between now and the time of our death.

A short time ago I saw a film on death. A man in middle years, married and with two daughters, was wrestling with terminal cancer and the fact of his approaching death. As the film progressed, we became aware that these were not actors on the screen, but a real family and the man was actually a cancer victim. Someone with only a few months to live had allowed a photographer to film him in his last tragic weeks! Believe me, the emotional impact of this real-life documentary was staggering.

Well, your death and mine are being filmed

right now. To not reckon with that is foolish, and we can start today to claim the future God has for each one of us. We cannot separate our present from our future. You are right now the person you are aiming to become. If you've ever driven a motorcycle, as I do, you can appreciate this principle. You do not steer a motorcycle going forty miles an hour—you aim it (this is probably true as well for a racing sailboat or a plane). When I'm driving down the road, I must look far ahead for turns, curves, other vehicles and aim for openings.

Life is like that. We fix our eye on something we feel to be our destiny and then aim at it. Faith means asking God to show us what we're meant to be or do and then aiming for it.

A friend of mine in middle years, when most of her contemporaries were settling for the status quo, began to dream about her own destiny. Betty lives in Bermuda and had a concern for young people with reading disabilities. There was no place on the island that offered help or correction for that special problem. So, Betty went off to Columbia University in New York and got her master's degree in the area of psychology that deals with corrective reading. Upon returning to Bermuda, she set up a clinic which has already helped hundreds of young people . . . their lives are different because of Betty.

Betty is proof that it is never too late to claim your destiny. We are not locked into our present. A businessman I know went through a serious nervous breakdown. Psychiatry did not prove especially helpful to him. The turning point came, however, when it was suggested that maybe he didn't like who he was and that his nervous breakdown was an attempt to die to the self that had always been. "What kind of person are you?" was the question that seemed to trigger something in him. "Well," he said, "I've always been a good old boy. Everybody takes advantage of me. I never get mad. I'm always around; always mopping up; always picking up the pieces." "Who would you like to be?" was the next question. Instantly he replied, "The bold one!"

Since this man believed that God could change a man's life, he claimed with God's help a new destiny and a new name. He was not stuck with being "a good old boy"; rather he saw himself as the bold one, the innovator, the initiator. This is how your sense of destiny can shape the future and help you to become the one and only you.

My dentist is a Roman Catholic who grew up in a home where the practice of that faith was very meaningful. In his early years he wanted to enter the priesthood. But when he learned the Roman Catholic doctrine of transsubstantiation (that the bread and wine of the mass become the body and blood of Christ), he felt unworthy to be a priest. Instead he studied science and ultimately entered dentistry. However, that original sense of destiny is still very much with him, and he is presently attending night school to learn psychology, which in his case will equip him as a kind of secular priest who can help bind the wounds of people.

In a profound sense we all become that at which we aim. You *are* your dreams. T. E. Lawrence says, "All men dream . . . but not equally. They who dream by night in the dusty recesses of their minds wake in the day to find that it is vanity; but the dreamers of the day are dangerous men, for they act out their dream with open eyes to make it possible."

On the day I was writing this, I learned that some research now being conducted proves that the things one sees in the mind's eye are as real as the things one sees out a window.

Both result from electrical impulses that reach the vision center of the brain, according to Walter Chase, director of research and head of the department of basic and visual science at the Southern California College of Optometry.

The daydreamer, vacantly staring out the window but seeing nothing except what he imagines, sees those imaginary scenes because the signals are transmitting what the mind's eye sees, Chase said. "There isn't much difference between the signals that are activated by the mind's eye and ones that are activated by the eye itself."[7]

I could not agree more. The Bible is full of this kind of daytime dreaming. The Apostle John writes, "I, John, saw a new heaven and a new earth." These daytime dreamers have the power to bring things into reality which change and shape the world.

I have lived for three years in Columbia, Maryland, a city that is literally the dream of two people, Jim and Libby Rouse. It is one of America's new "model cities." In his book, *A Nation of Strangers*, Vance Packard calls Columbia the most hopeful new city in the land. It came into being because Jim and Libby had their lives radically changed by God as participants in the Church of the Saviour in Washington, D.C.

Jim was an investment banker and a builder and developer of the new kind of shopping mall which is proliferating everywhere. At the time Jim and Libby lived in Baltimore and had a great concern for what was happening to people in both the inner city and the suburbs. They became interested in planning a city where people could become everything they were meant to be.

Over a number of months they met and talked with city planners, architects, theologians, psychologists, psychiatrists, and all kinds of people who were involved with the human experiment, personally and corporately. They put their dreams and the input from experts together and came up with a plan which is now Columbia. Now thirty thousand people live and work there.

In a sense we are all the products of persons who have dreamed about us and for us, and to some degree we have become what they dreamed. I recently interviewed a psychiatrist who is the administrative head of one of this country's great psychiatric research centers. When asked about his choice of profession, he said that fifty years ago his mother, to whom he was very attached and who had died in his arms, had a dream that he should become a doctor.

Freud had a great deal to say about the power of a mother or a father's dream in shaping the destiny of a child. Undoubtedly, many of us are today something of a projection of the dreams of our parents. And if you have children, your dreams are beginning to shape them. Sometimes our dreams for our children or our parents' dreams for us have been a detriment, but the point is that our dream about the future for someone else can become a powerful, shaping force.

Sorting out my own authentic dreams and goals from those inherited from others reminds me of one of my favorite stories. A man answering his doorbell admitted a visitor who was followed by a big shaggy dog. As they sat talking, the dog bumped into an end table sending a lamp crashing to the floor. After chewing on the rug for awhile the dog began to roam through the house, his progress marked by the sound of breaking glass. When finally he jumped on the sofa with his muddy feet and curled up for a nap the outraged householder was unable to contain himself any longer. "Don't you think you should have trained your dog better than that?" he burst out. "*My* dog?" exclaimed the visitor in surprise. "I thought it was *your* dog."

That story says a great deal to me about the things in our lives that need to be identified and reevaluated. We don't know how they got there. Perhaps it was through someone else's dreams. But there comes a time when we need to get life down to basics and begin to aim at some simple, clear, attainable goals that have our name on them. Let's get rid of all the "big dogs" that don't belong there.

Years ago a relative of mine who is extremely successful in one of America's larger corporations changed his life-style radically. He had gone up the executive ladder with great rapidity and for good reason. Knowledgeable and personable, each advance on the ladder brought a bigger home and more expansive living until he was finally in a large house alongside a golf course with matching Cadillacs in the driveway. With the ultimate promotion to vice president of the corporation, he and his wife realized they were being shaped by their success and were living in a style they really didn't enjoy. In a reversal of what looked like the inevitable role, they moved to a smaller house in a more modest neighborhood. They began to live more simply at the very time that they had attained the greatest influence and privilege and wealth.

In some measure we all have a grasp on our destiny. We are not the product of some corporate entity or some cultural force which is blindly pushing us. We can decide how we want to live

and where we want to live and go and do exactly
that. All along the way we have choices.

Listen to what John Barth wrote in *The Sot-
Weed Factor* about choosing "... Ah, God, it were
an easy matter to choose a Calling, had one all
time to live in! I should be fifty years a Barrister,
fifty a Physician, fifty a Clergyman, fifty a Sol-
dier! Aye, and fifty a Thief, and fifty a Judge.
All Roads are fine Roads, beloved Sister, none
more than another, so that with one Life to spend
I am a Man bare-bumm'd at Taylors with Cash
but for one pair of Breeches, or a Scholar at Book-
stalls with Money for a single Book; to choose ten
were no trouble; to choose one, impossible! All
Trades, all Crafts, all Professions are wondrous,
but none is finer than the rest together. I cannot
choose. . . ." [8]

To me this underscores a need for a simplified
sense of destiny. The alternative is a confusion so
crippling it crushes life in the present.

On a recent trip to Bermuda my wife and I took
off on our two bikes for a day's excursion. We
arrived at the old harbor in St. George's just in
time to see a most unusual sight. Five or six
grizzled commercial fishermen were gathered
around the wharf watching a young man shove
off in an old, clinker-built, double-ender sailboat
slightly over twenty feet long. The sails were
patched and the rigging looked worn. "You know
where that crazy buzzard is going?" one man vol-
unteered. "He's sailing to England in that thing."
And as the little boat pulled out from the harbor,
those veteran sailors shook their heads in scorn
and disbelief.

But somehow the sight of that one frail craft
with its lone crew stirred something deep inside
of me, and without meaning to, I found myself
waving and shouting, "Bon Voyage!" Surprised

and encouraged, the young captain waved back and continued to do so until the little boat was gone from sight.

For that young man, getting there wasn't the important thing. He didn't have to make it, but somehow he had to start out. He would not be the man that he was meant to be in the present if he didn't set his sights in the future for that ridiculous and seemingly impossible trip. And I think that's what life is all about. Whether we arrive or not at some future goal isn't the issue. It's O.K. to fail as long as you launch out. You dare not stay in the harbor or you will lose your soul and never discover the one and only you. At this point, let me give you a self-diagnosis test to help find the shape of risk, as you contemplate leaving your safe harbor and launching out into the deep.

Grade yourself in the blank before each question on a scale of zero to ten as you understand your potential in each of these areas. A score of ten will be the maximum, and zero, of course, is the minimum. To give yourself a ten does not mean that you are perfect, but that you believe you're living up to your full potential in that area at this time in your life. Do not think about your answers too long. Your instant reaction is probably the most accurate one.

_____ 1. I allow people to know me intimately, even though I am hurt at times.

_____ 2. I see positive things in other people and enjoy mentioning them.

_____ 3. I regularly use my time, influence, and money to help advance some cause or group I believe in.

_____ 4. I am able to surrender myself to God in the concrete things of daily life and to trust him with my assets, liabilities, and opportunities.

_____ 5. I feel fulfilled in who I am and what I'm doing. I am aware of using many of the gifts God has given me.

_____ 6. I am able and willing to pray. My prayer life is what it could be and what I want it to be.

_____ 7. I am able to study systematically. (Some of my regular reading is serious nonfiction.)

_____ 8. I can accept negative feelings and deal with them creatively (that is, I do not deny them, repress them or compulsively act on them).

_____ 9. I am motivated to carry out projects and assignments that are important to me.

_____10. I am able to deal with my fears. I can identify my fears and I am unafraid of fear.

_____11. I believe I have the gift of joy independent of how well things are going at the moment.

_____12. I can react to people and situations spontaneously and creatively as over against being rigid and stereotyped.

_____13. I feel I have the ability to communicate my ideas and feelings one to one or in groups so that I am understood.

_____14. I have specific goals for my future.

_____15. I have a love of adventure. I enjoy attempting new things even if I fail.

Go through this list of abilities and attitudes and check the three areas in which you gave yourself the lowest score. Copy these down and put them away someplace where you'll see them every day. Begin to claim them as the particular shape of your future and part of your unique destiny.

# 8

## *Enjoy Your Strengths*

WHEN I was twenty I shipped out as a deck hand on an ore boat on the Great Lakes for a summer. The captain was a very interesting character. It was difficult to understand exactly what skills had earned him the privileged position of captain on a Great Lakes ore boat. He didn't handle people well, and he didn't appear to be an especially able seaman. And unfortunately, he could not seem to inspire cooperation among his crew. But, one memorable day I discovered what his true skills were.

The fog was heavy all about us and all the boats in the shipping lane were creeping at a very slow pace, blowing their fog horns frequently. Our boat alone continued at full speed ahead. The captain's asset was that he dared to run that boat full speed ahead even in a fog when he couldn't see. (This was before the days of radar.) The season on the Great Lakes is limited and captains are hired in terms of how many round trips they can work in before the ice makes shipping impossible. I'm sure nobody, given the size and horsepower of our boat could have made more round trips than our captain. While he had many weaknesses, his strengths outweighed them and earned his captaincy.

In striving to discover the one and only you I think my old ship captain has a lesson for us. We hear so much about the importance of diversity these days that we take it seriously, in business and in our personal lives. In our attempts to be expert in many areas we can fall into the trap of reenacting man's first sin which was to be like God.

The book of Genesis gives us a description of a very intimate relationship between God and Adam and Eve in those early days. It was not a relationship of equals, but one where God and his human creations were friends who talked and talked in the garden at sunset each day.

In the story, the serpent enticed them to disobey God by eating the fruit they had been told to let alone with the promise that it would make them like God—knowing all things. Perhaps our desire to be complete and well rounded, self-sustained, and self-contained is related to that original desire of Adam and Eve to know everything—to be like God.

Obviously, this is not attainable, but there is something in me that continues to work toward this goal, and I think that is what original sin is largely all about. Something in me wants to admit no weaknesses—to be "all things to all people" in the worst possible sense. . . . I would like to be a great preacher and writer, counselor and administrator, evangelist and healer. Let me confess that in my fantasies I am the kind of person who electrifies and transforms people or situations simply by my presence.

But reality too often breaks in. In 1971 the Baltimore Colts, at the peak of their fame as Super Bowl Champions, issued me an invitation to come and lead morning worship before one of their games. I accepted immediately for two reasons: I would get two free tickets, and I thought this would give me a kind of vicarious sports greatness. Even if I could not play great football, I would, for the moment, be chaplain to a great football team.

My youngest son went with me, and meeting this great bunch of athletes was a high point for both of us and an experience we will never forget. But later on that afternoon at Memorial Stadium in Baltimore we saw the Colts get beaten by a far inferior team. Conversation was difficult on the way home. Mark and I had a hard time understanding how they could have played such inferior ball after having received such superior prayer.

When we got home, the wife of a dear friend called me. She's a great Colts fan and knew I had conducted their worship service that day. "Hey, Bruce," she said, "do me a favor, would you? If I'm ever sick, please don't come over and pray for me."

Now you see, much as I would like to picture myself as a man full of power, inspiring great deeds, one who can electrify a football team, I am reminded again and again to focus instead on the things I can do well—to do them and enjoy them.

I remember taking part in a renewal conference in a very famous old southern church. Fantastic things had begun to happen at every level of the congregation's life. People were being healed, lives were being changed, laymen were being called to the ministry, and clergy were being called to lay ministries. The pastor had been serving that church for forty years and had had this vision from the beginning. Talking to him over dinner, I asked why it had taken so long for this church to come alive. "Oh," he said, "that's no mystery. I just had to stay here long enough to bury all the people who were against renewal." His realistic appraisal impressed me. Instead of blaming himself for long years of failure, he had the tenacity to hang onto his dream and his faith and to stay long enough for God to bring it all to pass.

So, I am convinced that to discover the one and only you means you can stop working on your weaknesses. The best approach, I think, is the one used in Alcoholics Anonymous. The first step of their program is to get the drinker to admit that he or she is powerless over alcohol. The second step is to confess to another human being the inability to handle alcohol. And the third step is to turn the problem over to God.

It's as simple as that, and it works. They don't try to overcome their weaknesses. Rather, they confess their weakness and enjoy a fellowship with other people who are also weak. There is no pretense here. I think this is the whole dynamic of A.A. People are free to be themselves and to be weak people together.

There are implications and applications for all of us here. So often we have to pretend that we are strong people instead of accepting and even enjoying the fact that we are weak. Recently I read about twelve ministers and twelve psychiatrists who met for a two-day seminar on healing. A psychiatrist chaired the meeting, and he opened with these words, "We are all healers whether we are ministers or doctors. Why are we in this business? What is our motivation?"

After only ten minutes of intense discussion they came to total agreement: "We are in this business for our own healing." It is a powerful thing for somebody in the healing profession to admit that he is there for his own healing.

It seems to me the A.A's have a two-sided solution that has special application for us. They turn their problems over to God, but they also ask others for help. It's difficult enough for most of us to turn our problems over to God, but to ask somebody else for help—aye, there's the rub. As a matter of fact, our very weakness and our need to ask others for help inadvertently creates authentic fellowship. The true church cannot exist where everyone is strong. It is a mutual society of the weak helping the weak.

We have been conditioned to think of a great leader as one who can help the weak, but a broader and more effective kind of leadership is emerging where the weak are helping the weak and finding strength together.

On fall days I always watch for those marvelous overhead dramas when Canadian geese fly in "V" formation. As I understand it, there is not one lead goose. Rather, specialists in aerodynamics say that geese can fly so far and so long because each one helps the flock by taking his turn as leader.

In a wind tunnel, two engineers discovered what happens to the formation of geese. Each goose in flapping its own wings creates an upward lift for the following goose. This gives the whole flock seventy-one percent greater flying range than if each bird flew alone. Leadership is rotated because no goose can stay up there very long. If an individual goose falls back and begins to think, "Nobody will miss me in this crowd," he immediately feels the heavier load of flying alone and speeds up to get back into the formation. Bird fanciers seem to feel that those who fall behind are encouraged by the honking of their peers.

There is a significant application here for us. We can't stay way out in front alone for very long. But together, if we rotate leadership and begin to build on each other's weaknesses and help one another, we can extend the range and the scope of our spiritual journey.

For so long we have been conditioned to hide our weaknesses. We think we must live up to the role expected of us in each situation. For example, I have always been embarrassed by my ineptitude with figures and legal details. I learned early in our marriage that my wife has a knack for these things, and so, gradually, she took over handling our finances, doing our income taxes and keeping our checkbook. In those first years this was a threat to my masculinity, but long ago I came to realize that being able to handle money well and fill in government forms has nothing to do with maleness or femaleness. Now, I'm no longer embarrassed to say that my wife handles this in our family.

But, there are still so many things that I hang on to, refusing to admit defeat simply because they threaten my self-image or my male image. The American Management Association has a theory that has helped me immensely with this. They say there are basically two kinds of leaders in the world: the entrepreneur and the manager. The entrepreneur is the one able to start a whole new process, to find new ways of bringing together resources, new methods of manufacturing, marketing, and distributing. The manager is somebody who can take an existing enterprise and run it efficiently and profitably.

The American Management Association people say that it is a mistake when entrepreneurs become managers and, conversely, that managers will seldom become entrepreneurs. Successful growth occurs when entrepreneurs can entrepreneur and managers can manage.

If this is true in business, it is even more true in life. And yet how often I have glibly advised other people, "Well, you started that thing and you ought to finish it." This is really only a half-truth. In asking people who are entrepreneurs to stay and bring a thing through to successful conclusion, we are asking them to work in the area of their weakness. To evaluate which type you are, entrepreneur or manager, to accept that and go with it, can be a big part of the success of any enterprise.

If in discovering the one and only you, we can each do our own thing, working in the area of our strengths, we can reverse a process that has made victims of many of us. Forget about your weaknesses! Enjoy your strengths and practice them to the glory of God.

A friend of mine grew up in the hill country and claims he can barely read and write. But twenty years of service in the navy seemed to develop in him a keen ability to lead men. When he retired from the navy, he joined a new company and rose to a top leadership position in a short time. It doesn't matter that he reads haltingly and writes laboriously. He understands people and knows how to make them work together. This man has a talent beyond schoolroom skills that has put him in demand in business as an organizer and a leader.

Somehow we need to learn to maximize our strengths and minimize our weaknesses. I read an article in a hospital publication recently which tried to do just that in behalf of an institution which is the target for much criticism today. The medical profession, and hospitals in particular, are under attack because of their costs. The public is resentful of doctors' fees and hospital bills. The writer of this article says, "Yes, there are money changers in the hospital temples. Fees are exorbitant and many doctors are bent on ever increasing fees." But he goes on to say, "The church, by comparison, sits as a wistful void in which infrequent worshippers, bowed in pews or before candlelit shrines, are comforted chiefly by the longing and the love in their own natures. Their priests are in the streets: Father Groppis invading legislatures, Berrigan brothers accused of political plottings, sisters thrilled to be involved in intrigue—all famished for a temporal martyrdom. Not even voices from the Vatican, tinged now with worldly advice to rulers of momentary power, speak with the tones of eternity and enduring compassion."

He continues, "It is from the emergency department of the great hospital that a voice is heard: 'Come unto me, all ye . . .' The disheveled girl screaming from a bad trip with dope, brought struggling between policemen to whom we assign our harshest tasks while reviling them; she is one.

"The young black father comforting his child who has waked in a waiting room chair to cry, 'I want my mommie'; he is one. The hot rodder, smashed and bleeding; he is one.

"The acolytes and ministrants of the great hospital do not ask: 'Of our faith? Of our party?'"

He goes on to say, "Beside the great hospital, how vain and shallow the universities have become. They neither learn nor teach, as they once did, of the relationship to exaltation of the spirit that is to be found in the nonsectarian search for an understanding of the exquisite nature of things and men. They have become pits of confusion dominated by trivial men and women intoxicated by a false sense of superior and special enlightenment and driven by petty ambitions for self. They offer a life infected by mincing dilettantes.

"By contrast, in hospitals at every hour the dedicated study and teach: experienced physicians, closely followed by resident and intern, aided by orderlies and nurses, come swiftly to serve. In great hospitals man has created for himself machines that combat encroaching death. When the cry of pain is heard a hundred skilled hands, a hundred compassionate faces, move to help, by darkness or by day. The great doors are never shut." [9]

I do not quote this writer because I am necessarily in agreement with him. But this is a brilliant example of the strategy we're talking about of maximizing strengths and minimizing weaknesses. He admits questionable profits are being made, but he goes on to say where else can you find so dependable a source of help!

A man I know is a professor at a great university. He and his wife have a group meeting weekly in their home. These young couples are struggling with the whole business of discovering who they really are.

The professor wrote me recently because the group had been studying *Ask Me to Dance,* a book of mine that deals with becoming a whole person. They had come up with an innovative exercise which I thought was exciting. Each person in the group wrote a letter of recommendation for himself or herself. It was suggested that they address that letter to a deacon in their church or to me. They were to imagine that they were applying for a position on a team being formed for the purpose of helping people to become whole. Copies of those letters were enclosed in the letter the professor wrote me and I'd like to share some excerpts from them with you.

Dear Sir:

. . . I guess my gift is being able to create an atmosphere in which people can have some stretching experiences but not feel threatened. I have done this with all the adults in church school on two occasions . . . If you can use me in a way where these skills are needed, I'd really like to work with you.

Dear Sir:

I would like to recommend myself on the past experience I've had in the following fields and the successes I've had. I would like to be able to exert my humor on those who refuse to smile or laugh at themselves. Maybe I could get them to laugh at me, then with me, then we could laugh together . . . I'm very aware that you have had many qualified applicants, but if you could please give me a personal interview I'm sure that my good grooming and sex appeal would be an asset to your program.

P.S. I can also type and do some bookkeeping.

Dear Sir:

How would you like to have at your disposal a "together" kind of person to assist you in your work? This letter is a recommendation of myself to fill that role . . . Some of the strengths I've been awakened to are creativity with groups in leading people to discover their own value as persons. I've learned to be real and vulnerable in a group situation. I am sensitive to what's going on verbally and nonverbally.

Dear Sir:

. . . I am willing to do whatever is necessary, go anywhere, work for anybody. I am a worker more than a thinker although I do have a logical bent and can usually provide solutions to problem solving. I believe I have a better than average sense of humor but also am able to contemplate serious points. I have ability in organization and demonstrate leadership when required . . . I have a feeling of warmth toward most all people, I admit to mixed feelings toward some, but generally can get along well with 95 percent of those I come in contact with. So with fear and trembling I submit myself to this work should you accept me.

Dear Sir:

. . . I can share where it hurts—I enjoy playing with people—I can cry with them too—I am willing to fail—I affirm those about me—I am an active listener—I stick to the job till it is complete—I am friendly and outgoing—I am intelligent—I am creative—I am flexible.

These people are learning to enjoy their strengths and to make the most of them to the glory of God. Now, I'd like to suggest that you think of a job or assignment that you'd like to have. Do what the people in this group have done. Write a letter of recommendation listing only your strengths and tell why you think you are uniquely qualified for that particular position. If your sense of humility hinders you from writing such a letter, just remember it's the Creator who has given you these abilities and these strengths and it's O.K. to take pride in them.

Knowing your strengths and enjoying them are an important part of discovering the one and only you.

# 9

## The Gift of Hope

WE WERE talking about our children. This is not unusual for parents and as I recall, in this case, the conversation went careening around between overwhelming pride and total despair. To be the parent of teenagers is to know both.

Suddenly my friend said to me, "What gift would you most like to give to your kids?" The words that came out of my mouth surprised me more than they did my friend. "I would want them to have the gift of hope."

I believe that hope profoundly shapes our view of the world around us, and next to faith it is, perhaps, the most essential factor in discovering the one and only you. This is the gift I would like to give my children . . . the gift of hope. A gift that would enable them to meet each day confident that good things are ahead; that they are adequate; that they can handle whatever comes.

Recently, I've made a personal reexamination of the gift of hope. The Bible speaks of a troika of faith, hope, and love and links the three together inseparably. Yet in the past I know I have talked and thought a great deal more about the gifts of faith and love than I have about the gift of hope.

I now see that hope is a coefficient of faith. In Hebrews 11:1 the writer talks about faith being "the substance of things hoped for." That says to me that faith, unless it is coupled with the gift of hope, will produce nothing. Faith is believing that God can make happen what we hope for. Without hope faith is sad and ineffective.

Actually, life without hope is a dreadful thing. It makes each day a desert and the future dark and foreboding. In the June 21, 1973, issue of *The Washington Post* I read about the desperate drought in West Africa: "In the northern part of the Republic of Niger, up toward the Algerian and Libyan borders, about 100,000 Tuaregs are waiting for something which for them is worse than death—the end of their old way of life. They cling to the handful of camels and goats left to them and wait for the rain, which in other years has made the desert bloom into pasture in three days. But after seven years of drought, which has affected much of West and Central Africa, the seeds of the sparse desert grass are scorched and dead.

". . . On most days, a truck or a Land Rover gets up here with food: nothing for the animals, and about a half pound of milk powder or a pound of sorghum for the people. The milk gives the children diarrhea. There were only four cows to be seen in a 400-mile tour. They were eating asses' dung.

". . . 'How can you tell them that the seeds are too scorched to grow any pasture?' says Christina van der Velle, a Belgian woman who works with a U.N. nomad aid program. 'If the rain comes, the food trucks will not get through to them, and there will be no food for them and no food for the animals either.' " [10]

An individual life without hope is like an unrelieved wasteland which cannot revive even if rain comes. You see, if there is no hope, even a rainfall of good things—a gift of money or friendship—brings no hope, for there are no seeds within to spring to life.

Life without hope in Niger is understandable in the face of their crucial situation. But hopelessness does not always depend on our situation. Recently a student at Northwestern was trying to describe to me the radical shift in the youth scene in the last few years. "Youth on college campuses today," he said, "no longer even rebel. A kind of paralysis has set in. Today's youth believes in no belief. They are no longer even against anything. There is no suicide, for suicide implies being against life. There is not even a death wish. There is simply vast unrelieved hopelessness in the heart of many of our young people today."

Hopelessness can attack the people of God as well. One can be a Christian without hope and one can have hope without being a Christian. Listen to this poignant statement by Dr. C. Adrian Heaton, President of the American Baptist Seminary of the West, speaking about the plight of many of the clergy today: "All the world's a stage and we are desperately under-rehearsed. Week after week we ministers are pushed headlong onto the stage to play our roles. We gaze about and see strange mind-expanding scenes. We recite our theologies written for other days, and people are bored. We act out liturgies of piety but the world is amused. We use tender gestures of self-giving love as expresions of our social concerns but our congregations sense that we have too little, too late. We pray for the floodlights above us to be darkened so that our humiliation may be hid but the candle-power is doubled. We rush toward the exits and find them locked."[11]

How then can we receive the gift of hope? I think it comes best by simply believing in God, his goodness, his power, his love, his infinite concern for each of our lives. We trust God to work not only in our personal affairs, but in the affairs of all people. At the very heart of the familiar verse, "We know that in everything God works for good with those who love him, who are called according to his purpose," is the gift of hope. It is the gift of hope in a God big enough to use the most devious designs of men to accomplish his ends.

The Bible is full of incredible tales of hope in the midst of desperate situations. We find Joseph, the favorite of his father, sold into slavery by his eleven brothers. First, they plotted to kill him but decided instead to make a little profit on him. Years later when he has become the number two man in Egypt, second only to the pharaoh, his brothers come to him from the famine-parched land of his father. When he reveals himself to them, they are terrified, certain that their brother will kill them or refuse to help them. But having the gift of hope, Joseph says to his brethren, "Don't worry. You meant it for evil, but God meant it for good."

This is what the gift of hope is all about. It doesn't mean that his brothers didn't sin and would not have to atone and repent for that sin. But because Joseph had the gift of hope, their sins could not ultimately hurt him. He was beyond being resentful, vengeful, or vindictive.

In Genesis we read a similar story about Abraham. When Abraham led that amazing procession out of Ur of the Chaldees in search of the promised land, he was accompanied by his nephew, Lot. After many years and unbelievable adventures, they finally arrive at Canaan. But by this time, bickering has developed among the families of Lot and Abraham. Abraham, the older man, the leader, the one to whom all honor should have come, turns to Lot and says, "You choose the land you want, and I'll take what's left." Lot immediately chooses the lush plains of Sodom and Gomorrah, and Abraham is left with the hard, rocky, upland places for his family and his herds.

Only Abraham's gift of hope could explain this astounding scene. He believes in a God who can put him where he wants him in spite of the selfish choice of an ungrateful nephew.

The gift of hope affects life at every level. Recently the Pittsburgh Steelers football team won their first divisional championship in forty years. One newspaper reporter in an interview with the Steelers' owner asked this question, "What made the difference this year?" The owner replied, "Our players believe in themselves now. Last year our team was about as good as this year's, but the players didn't think they could win. They just waited to get beat. This year the players believe in themselves, so do the newspapers, the coaches, and the owner. Everybody in Pittsburgh is a believer now." [12]

The owner of the Steelers was talking about the gift of hope. Which team wins? Not necessarily the better team, because in pro football most are about equal in size, talent, experience, and equipment. It is the intangible, elusive quality of hope that makes one of these teams a winner. But there is more to hope than winning, though I am convinced it is often the extra ingredient that makes a person or team a winner.

The gift of hope makes a dramatic difference in our life-style whether we win or lose. When I was a student at Princeton Seminary, I spent weekends serving a church in a small town on the Hudson River—a church so small they couldn't afford a real preacher, so they settled for me.

The vitality of that church, though, was in the people who understood what it meant to be the people of God and who exercised this ministry. Mrs. K. was one of these people.

Through correspondence courses she had learned as much about the Bible as most preachers. And if someone was in trouble, Mrs. K. heard about it and was there.

I've been gone from that parish for over twenty years, but I visited Mrs. K. in a nursing home just before she died. There she was, in what I hope is a dying breed of nursing homes—an old converted house never meant for that purpose. I made my way up creaky stairs, through bad odors and decaying people, and finally found her. Still exercising her ministry to others, she had four or five friends gathered around to hear the opera on her little radio. Every Saturday afternoon, it seems, she was hostess for the opera and could explain what was happening to her guests.

I said, "Hey, Mrs. K. It's your old preacher." Interrupting her party, she took me aside for a chat. Long a diabetes sufferer, she was now totally blind. When I asked how things were going, I discovered that her husband had died and she was penniless and a welfare patient in the home, but she was radiant as she always had been.

"You know, Bruce," she said, "it's so wonderful here. If I don't feel like making my bed in the morning, they make it for me. All my meals are fixed for me, and if I ask them, they do my laundry. God is so good."

Remembering what an avid reader she had always been, I asked, "Mrs. K., do you miss your sight?" "Oh, yes," she said, "but you know, Bruce, I just remember all the wonderful things I've seen during my lifetime. Why, would you believe it, I went to the New York World's Fair *three* times!"

Mrs. K. is gone now, but not really. She is part of that great cloud of witnesses. With none of the externals of life that we think of as God's blessings, she still rejoiced and believed in him.

That memorable visit reminded me of the scene from the play *The Unsinkable Molly Brown* where Molly sings "I Ain't Down Yet." And this ought to be the cry everywhere. To believe that God is with you in your present extremities. To say in your joy and sadness: Everything isn't over yet. There is more to come, and I ain't down yet.

How do we communicate this gift of hope to others? Usually in simple, nonverbal ways. When we moved to Columbia, a friend of mine, a man about my age, shared some advice his doctor had given him. It seems that to stay alert and keen in the middle years we all need to have a little danger in our lives. The doctor personally had taken up flying and was convinced that an hour or two a week in the sky was making him a better doctor, husband, and, in fact, a better man.

That seemed a wonderful excuse for doing what I had wanted to do for years, and so I bought a motorcycle. After some shopping around with my fifteen-year-old son, we settled on the smallest full-sized motorcycle that Honda makes, a Trail 90. This meant that my son could use the motorcycle to ride in the woods around our house, and I would have an economical and adventurous way to travel the six miles to and from my office.

Well, it's no small matter getting a motorcycle licensed and registered, not to mention passing the test for your personal license. But the great day finally came, and I was ready for my maiden run to the office. Wearing my best business suit and tie and with my briefcase strapped on behind, I started out.

Needless to say, I was terrified and full of anxieties. Would I make it in the real world as a motorcyclist? Since about one-half mile of the journey entailed traveling on a four-lane superhighway, I picked a late morning hour so that I would not get into heavy traffic. All went well, and by the time I reached the highway I was moving along at a speedy thirty-five miles per hour. Suddenly, coming at me in the opposite direction at about seventy miles an hour was what motorcyclists refer to as the "ultimate machine." It was a huge Honda 750 carrying a burly young cyclist with his girl hanging on behind, both in black leather jackets, long hair flowing out from under each helmet.

As we were about to pass each other, the driver raised his left arm in the "ride on" salute that motorcyclists give. I cautiously looked around to see who was following me and discovered that I was the only vehicle on the road. Obviously he meant me! I had been accepted into that great fellowship of easy riders "my first time out." Timidly I gave him back a "ride on" as he whisked by. I couldn't believe that getting into this mysterious fraternity would be so easy. Simply by spending several hundred dollars for a tiny machine I was one of them—no questions asked.

While returning home from the office that night, I looked for other motorcycles. Spotting one a great way off and before the driver could even see me clearly, I greeted him with the "ride on" sign which he loyally returned. Since then, whenever I ride, I find our special fellowship quick to greet one another.

I will always be grateful for the gift of hope given to me by my unknown donor that first day out on the road. It did something for my self-confidence and for my ego. It was a priceless gift.

We parents need to learn creative nonverbal ways to communicate the gift of hope to our children. At dinner one night a close friend was reminiscing about his childhood during the Great Depression. His stepmother had an abundance of the gift of hope, and at the time when the family was the poorest, she went out and bought herself a new hat, much to the despair of her thrifty husband. But that hat said something to the rest of the family. It communicated her hope that things were going to get better.

There is no way that you and I can become the

one that God meant us to be unless we let him give us the gift of hope. The funeral of a friend was held in Pittsburgh a few months ago. He was a man whose life was touched by God and because of him many people in that city found hope and a fresh beginning.

As the coffin was being taken from the church, the organist began the recessional hymn chosen by his widow, "The Impossible Dream" from *Man of La Mancha.* How appropriate! He had lived the impossible dream, and now, in death, his family and friends could affirm that. To all of us the gift of hope can bring about that impossible dream, for this life and beyond.

# 10

## Give Hope Away

NOT LONG ago I read an item in the paper about a tragic incident in Los Angeles: An unidentified man was killed at dawn today on the Hollywood Freeway after being hit by five cars."

The police said the man was knocked to the pavement by a car which did not stop. He regained his feet and was hit by a second car which also sped off. He got up again and was hit by a third car which sped off. And, believe it or not, he got up once more and was hit by a fourth car which failed to stop. Then, while sprawled on the ground, he was run over by a fifth car which also continued on.

It's unthinkable that five people could be so callous and uncaring and irresponsible. Yet perhaps this is only an advanced symptom of our time. To a lesser degree, all of us are hit-and-run drivers (or victims) on life's daily freeway.

How many of you have been at a social, professional, or religious gathering where you've spent the evening with a succession of people who seem to run over you with their experiences and convictions and then ricochet off to somebody else? At the end of the evening you feel used, abused, and without a sense of worth. I'm beginning to see that in any encounter, casual or intense, where I fail to give away the gift of hope I am a relational hit-and-run driver on the freeway of life.

I believe that you and I can live our lives in such a way that people around us will know that we are aware of *their* worth and *their* potential and *their* uniqueness. Even those of us who have had a genuine experience of God often convey quite the opposite. All too often, though, we regale people with *our* spiritual experiences or *our* theology, all of which may be good and true, but it all has a selfish ring.

One hot spring day I was driving to work on my motorcycle and crossing a bridge near a great swamp. Suddenly, I had to swerve to avoid hitting a big box turtle sitting in the middle of the road. Eager to be a St. Francis and save the life of my hard-shelled friend, I stopped and went back to pick him up and move him off the road. But in the midst of my good deed for the day I changed my mind. I decided instead to play a trick on him, so I put him in my pocket and took him to the office.

All day long he was the center of attention. Beautiful secretaries, busy executives, and assorted visitors all fussed over him. He sat in air-conditioned splendor eating bacon, bread, peanut butter, and lettuce.

The staff eats lunch together at the office, and on this particular day a friend joined us and brought her guitar. So, along with everything else, he heard beautiful music, great singing, and all the while continued to stuff his little belly full of exotic foods.

That night at five o'clock I brought him back to the same place in the road where I found him, carried him to the side, and headed him back toward the swamp. And then it hit me. I wondered what kind of a tale he would tell his friends. How could he communicate to them the wonders of air-conditioning, the topography and geography of a modern office building, the experience of being surrounded by beautiful girls, and of eating strange foods and hearing wonderful music? I'm sure that from that time on he was known as "Crazy Charlie" to all the other turtles in the swamp. There is no way that the experience he had could ever be communicated to his friends.

Crazy Charlie is like many people who have had a dramatic conversion or a mountaintop experience of ecstasy or glimpsed a moment of profound truth. They try to relate that experience to people who have no equipment for understanding it and often they simply alienate others and minimize their own credibility. This is not the way to call forth the gift of hope.

Hope is an indispensable ingredient in becoming the one and only you, but the only way you can have the gift of hope is by giving it away. It is not a gift that you can contain and keep to yourself.

As I see it, the gift of hope affects both the subject and the object. I met a young clergyman recently who had been assigned by his bishop to meet my plane and drive me to a conference. I had never met him before, so as we drove along we were making conversation. I asked him what kind of a church he had. His answer was instant and electric: "I have a terrible church. I've had it for eight years and I keep asking my bishop to move me, but he never does. I can't stand it any more." "What's wrong with it?" I asked. "My church is full of Archie Bunkers," he responded. "Have you ever watched 'All in the Family'?" I replied that it was my favorite TV program.

"Then you'll know what I mean. I've got a blue-collar congregation full of cautious, bigoted, reactionary people who equate God with the American military-industrial complex and WASP values."

For the next few minutes my new friend delivered one of the strongest sermons against the "silent majority" I'd ever heard. That's all I remember of our conversation.

Several months later an old friend dropped by to see me. He had taken a new church. When I asked about it Howard immediately replied, "It's an exciting church. I can't wait to see what God is going to do with it." He described his congregation enthusiastically. "It's a church full of Archie Bunkers. I've never known much about this segment of America before, but I find that there is pure gold beneath their many defense mechanisms. They really are the core of America's greatness. They have tremendous courage; they work hard; they're faithful, loyal people. I'm discovering that their fear, defensiveness, and conservatism are the result of cultural, economic, and social pressures. I believe with all my heart that if God can touch some of these people, our church will come alive and become a mighty force in our town and in our denomination."

Now, I don't have to be very wise or prophetic to guess which of these two churches will thrive and feel the fresh winds of God's spirit blowing through it and which one will decline in faith and enthusiasm. What will make the difference? The real issue seems to be, which church contains the real Archie Bunker?

These two congregations seem basically the same, filled with "cautious, bigoted, reactionary people." But one pastor brings to the situation the gift of hope. He can see invisible qualities in his congregation, and with this vision of hope he will be able to call forth the real Archie Bunker, the Archie Bunker that the other pastor is unable to see. My guess is that the other pastor will live in despair and discouragement until his bishop finally moves him. But, even more tragic, unless he receives the gift of hope somewhere along the way, he will always be the pastor of a "terrible" church.

The gift of hope can affect all of life in concrete ways. I have been having serious problems with my teeth, and my dentist finally advised me to go to a specialist in gum disease. Well, the man my dentist recommended had excellent credentials and was a skilled mechanic besides. But, unfortunately, he was a man without hope. He told me I had come to him too late, that my prior dentist had failed me, that my medical doctor was probably failing me, and that my present dentist wasn't helping much.

After some months of treatment by this specialist, I said to my regular dentist, "Can't you recommend somebody else? I can't take this guy. He depresses me. I don't want someone to lie to me, but I want a man who has some hope for my teeth and who can call forth some hope in me." At this point in my life a second periodontist has just finished a laborious eighteen months working on my mouth. I don't think he is technically better than my first dentist, but he knows how to relate to people like me who are in despair. These days, whether I'm buying a car, life insurance, or dental care, I look for somebody who can give me the gift of hope.

As we've said, you have to have hope to give it away. You cannot give away what you don't have any more than you can come back from some place you haven't been. But, having received the gift of hope, there are some things that can help us transmit that gift to others or elicit it from others.

1. *Believe in the other person's worth.* This is a fundamental attitude that God can give us along with the gift of hope. If we believe that we have worth, then we have to believe that the person we are now involved with also has worth and potential.

A friend of mine is the head of a very flourishing manufacturing company. He is a keen and sensitive person whose life has been changed by

God through small groups. Each Christmas he gives his customers and special friends a beautiful art calendar with photographs or paintings of American scenery.

One of these hangs in my office and it reflects my friend Carl's philosophy in this way. Across the top is printed "Created especially for" and in huge block letters, BRUCE LARSON. Then, in very small print, it gives the name of the manufacturing company.

Each time I look at the calendar I know that I am special to my friend and his company. The calendar is not a means of promoting the name of his company. It says rather that his company knows my name and thinks I'm important.

One man's hope can have far-reaching effects on all of society. John Woolman, an amazing Christian who lived in the eighteenth century, had great passion and zeal, but he also had the gift of hope and knew how to call forth hope in others. Woolman was a Quaker, and at that time many wealthy Quakers were slaveholders. As a young man, he vowed to rid the Society of Friends of this terrible blight, and for thirty years he gave his life to that task.

Now John Woolman's strategy was basic and unique. He did not picket or hold mass rallies. He didn't publish vindictive sermons against slavery and those who practiced it. Rather over those thirty years he traveled up and down the length of the land visiting with slaveholders. He would simply accept their hospitality and ask them questions about how it felt as a child of God and a Christian to own slaves. There was no condemnation in his approach. He believed these slaveholders were responsible people of conscience, and he asked them disturbing questions: "What does the owning of slaves do to you as a moral person?"

"What kind of an institution are you passing on to your children?"

And so, he called forth something noble in the hearts of those Quakers. One hundred years before the Civil War not a single Quaker held slaves. This was the result of one man's social passion coupled with his own gift of hope and his ability to communicate that hope.

2. *Believe in the other person's future.* Recently I was interviewing the chief clinical psychologist for a statewide research project. He and his staff work with chronic alcoholics or young people who have a terminal illness.

When I asked my friend, "What do you, as a clinical psychologist, think wholeness looks like?" here is what he answered: "I think it has a lot to do with a sort of basic faith in the goodness of life. If I can get the person to face into his life and accept whatever the next day brings with a sense of hopefulness, with a feeling that there is meaning to his experience and his existence and that he is on some kind of a path toward growth, I have succeeded. And, hopefully, that might include some concept of the deity of God.

"And then if he can go at least halfway; make the effort to reach out to life; there is a paradox here—that if he will take responsibility for himself and his decisions and where he is ... if he just reaches out toward life—just to meet the fundamental responsibilities—things will unfold for him. I know that's a very weird description, but that's what I'm into these days. It's really strange."

I couldn't believe my ears. This gifted, trained psychologist realizes that he has no greater gift to give others than to believe in them and their future. To have hope for them means that they will begin to discover their own hope and to claim it.

I suppose this underlies all the effective work with people at any level. I recently heard of an inner city, integrated church that was absolutely brim full at every service and where people were finding help and hope and change. The pastor was asked the secret of his ministry. "Oh, it's no secret," he said. "I simply tell people who they are!"

Ideally every pastor ought to be able to do this in the pulpit. He ought to be able to tell people who they are and to have hope that the great days are ahead and to live in that kind of personal, positive eschatology.

3. *Believe in the other person's possibilities.* Don't feel it's all up to you. Even more important than transmitting hope is eliciting hope.

I attended a Bible study recently, and the teacher was talking about the conversation in Genesis 4 between Cain and God. Cain had just killed his brother Abel and God asked him, "Where is your brother?" Cain answered, "How do I know. Am I my brother's keeper?"

The teacher went on to say that in the Bible the Hebrew word for "keeping" *always* refers to animals, *never* to people. So when Cain responds to God about "keeping," he knew that he was not meant to be in the business of "brother keeping." And yet, so much of our theology about relationships has to do with "brother keeping." "Brother keeping," you see, is always patronizing. It puts one person in a superior position to another. It makes one the giver and the other the receiver, whether of food, money, advice, or hope.

The giving of hope to people has very little to do with being our brother's keeper. It has a great deal to do with being our brother's brother.

Father Damien, a Roman Catholic priest, served for years by his own choice in the leper colony of Molokai in Hawaii. He customarily began his Sunday morning sermons with the words, "My brothers and sisters." But on the Sunday after he contracted leprosy, he began with "We lepers . . ." Until that week he had led as one who had come to help lepers, but now his ministry was different. From that point on he was locked in and irrevocably committed to his congregation. They were equals. As equals, he could share in the gift of hope and call forth that gift in others.

4. *Believe in the other person's judgment.* Perhaps there is no better way to call forth hope than to believe in the other person's wisdom. How much we need to practice this in all our relationships.

One church has adopted a new rule for all official board meetings. No one is allowed to speak against another person's recommendation until he has said three good things about it. What a marvelous rule that would be for every family, every committee, every staff. First affirm the other person's judgment by saying three good things about his suggestion or recommendation. After that you are permitted to give reasons why you might be against it.

To immediately oppose a person's suggestion, even though your reasons are sound, is to say to that person that he is stupid and that he doesn't count.

A cartoon I saw recently portrayed an executive presiding at a staff meeting. This very pompous man with a scowl on his face is saying to his colleagues around the conference table, "The report is, of course, largely my work. But I don't want that to inhibit you. Run through it with a fine tooth comb. If you find any flaws don't hesitate to speak up because, make no mistake, this report will affect us all. I don't intend doing anything childish like putting it to the vote, but anyone not in favor should stand up now so that we can ... *see his stupid face!*"[13]

How often I have responded in just that smug, superior, put-down way to friends, colleagues, my children, my wife.

To discover my uniqueness I must give myself away recklessly, lavishly. For you to become the one and only you that God intended you must do the same. The greatest gift you have to give is yourself. The gift of hope comes from being reconciled to your past, fulfilled in your present, and having a sense of destiny about your future.

The Bible says that if you or I would save our life we will lose it. But, if we would give it away with abandon, lavishly, recklessly, we will save our lives. This is how to become the one and only you.

# Notes

1. C. S. Lewis, *Mere Christianity* (New York: Macmillan Company, 1960).

2. Alvin Toffler, *Future Shock* (New York: Random House, 1970).

3. John Gardner, *Self-Renewal* (New York: Harper & Row, 1965).

4. *Washington Post*, 16 April 1973.

5. Hermann Hesse, *Siddhartha* (New York: New Directions, 1922).

6. *Washington Post*, 15 May 1973.

7. *Los Angeles Times*, 16 August 1973.

8. John Barth, *The Sot-Weed Factor* (New York: Grosset, 1960).

9. *Pittsburgh Press*, 6 August 1972.

10. *Washington Post*, 21 June 1973.

11. C. Adrian Heaton quoted in thesis by The Reverend Lee Roy Brandes.

12. *Los Angeles Times*, December 1972.

13. *Washington Post*, 9 October 1972.